How to
Discipline
Without
Feeling Guilty

How to Discipline Without Feeling Guilty

Assertive Relationships with Children

Melvin L. Silberman, Ph.D.
and
Susan A. Wheelan, Ph.D.

RESEARCH PRESS
2612 North Mattis Avenue
Champaign, Illinois 61820

To my wife, Shoshana, and our children, Steven, Lisa, and Gabriel Silberman, who have supported my wish to be a strong and loving parent.

To my father, Daniel O'Connell Whoolan, Jr., who has taught me that it is possible to be a strong and loving parent.

Contents

Preface

This book is based on the fundamental conviction that *the rais ing and teaching of children requires strong, confident adults in charge of their homes and classrooms.* Children need adults who are their leaders, not their followers, adults who act rather than react, adults who assume authority instead of abdicate it. Parents, teachers, and anyone else in charge of children have little cause to feel guilty about regulating children's lives.

We further believe that adults do not have to be mean to mean business. There is a wide range of steps they can take to help children, in turn, take their demands seriously. With none of these steps do adults appear nasty, frightening, or villainous. In fact, rather than seem like some cruel ogre, an adult who uses these steps gains respect and trust.

The purpose, then, of *How to Discipline without Feeling Guilty*, is to help you acquire the confidence and skill of an adult in charge of children. Please be assured, however, that this book is not another attempt to get you to be a master technician, a wise psychologist, or a patient saint. You do not have to become any of these people for our advice to be effective. Becoming aware of a few aspects of your relationship with children, learning a small number of techniques, and changing some of the ways in which you typically solve conflicts is all that is suggested.

What we have to tell you stems as much from our personal experience as child caretakers as it does from our professional activity as parent and teacher trainers, school consultants, and psychotherapists. One or both of us has been a parent, a surrogate parent, an elementary school teacher, a high school teacher, and a group home worker. We have coped with the problems of child care as you have—seeking advice from friends, relatives, and colleagues; making tough decisions; and living with our actions for better or for worse. The joys and frustrations of being in charge of children are not unknown to us. We have also learned from our personal experience with children that the advice in books for parents and teachers tends to be too vague, too narrow, too permissive, or too time-consuming to really make a difference. For these reasons alone, this book was in our thoughts for several years before one word was ever written.

Conducting assertion training groups over the past eight years has paved the way to the writing of this book. Initially, our focus (and the focus of the vast majority of assertion trainers) was adult-to-adult communication. We helped people assert themselves with everyone from a spouse to an encyclopedia salesman, from a supervisor or boss to an auto mechanic. People came to our workshops from a variety of professions (doctors, lawyers, managers, policemen, business people) looking for responsible ways to relate to adults in stressful situations. Surprisingly, though, the relationships which brought the most pain to these adults were those with children. Time and time again, participants' problems with children arose. Complaints such as "I can't talk with her" and "He doesn't listen to me" were all too frequent.

Thus, we began to view assertion training as a format to help people deal more effectively not just with other adults but also with children. Some of the elements we emphasized were similar to those used in dealings between adults: respect for self and others, direct communication, keeping conflict focused and solvable. Some elements, however, were missing: How do assertive adults cope with children's dependence and immaturity? How do assertive adults adjust to children's growing capacity for autonomy? How do assertive adults work together to create a unified, yet flexible authority system in the home and in school? Thinking and experimentation about power relationships, developmental changes, and family and classroom systems had to be done to adapt assertion training for the specific needs of parents and teachers.

Over a period of time, in groups composed of people with varying concerns and later in groups geared especially for parents and teachers, the ideas and strategies outlined in this book took shape. We hope that the result of our search for assertive ways to relate to children will enable you to discipline with less guilt, to be in charge with less strife, and to provide them with the security and strength that they so clearly need.

Acknowledgments

We are indebted to the many parents and teachers whose ideas and experiences have become a part of this book.

Our special thanks go to:

Miriam Spector, whose ideas, thoughtful critiques, and editing skills have been invaluable.

Effie Bastas, Doug Crawford, Deana Katz, Tom Klee, Marci Resnick, and Marion Tallon, whose careful reviews provided direction for our work.

Alice Jackson and Geri Ball, who patiently guided us through the preparation of this book.

How to
Discipline
Without
Feeling Guilty

1 | The Willingness to Be in Charge

Is the exercise of adult authority damaging to children? That is the impression we have been given all too often. Book after book, friend after friend has told us that to impose direction on children is harmful. The use of authority, it is alleged, stifles creativity and emotional growth. Children, we are assured, can make wise choices for themselves with only gentle guidance. Moreover, we have been warned that children will resent us and eventually rebel against our values and beliefs if we control and restrict their activity too much. Some popular psychologists have even suggested to us that dealing with children can be viewed as an enterprise among equal partners; conflicts can be solved through negotiation. Finally, if all of the above appeals have not worked, we have been asked to consider the scars of our own childhood. Whatever timidity, anxiety, or lack of self-esteem we might currently possess is blamed on our parents' and teachers' use of authority.

There is some truth to these arguments. But they take on real meaning only if we understand the word *authority* to be synonymous with "autocrat" or "power monger." Assuming authority does not have to mean being *authoritarian*. It can mean, instead, *the willingness to be in charge.* The difference between parents and teachers who are authoritarian and those who are willing to be in charge has to do with the attitude of each toward authority. Authoritarian adults are eager to preserve their own power more than anything else, and thus are likely to use it oppressively. Adults who are willing to be in charge of children are equally concerned with understanding and helping them, and therefore are more likely to use their authority responsibly.

To be in charge requires parents and teachers to *deny, demand,* and *delegate.* It is saying no when children want things from us which we feel are unreasonable. It is saying "do this" when something is needed for the benefit of the child or others. And it is saying to children "go ahead and take some charge of your own life" when we believe that the value of risking freedom and exploration outweighs the security and wisdom of adult direction.

Authority viewed in this way is not psychologically damaging. In fact, it is as necessary as hugging and loving our children. There are several reasons for saying this. Every kind of group has to be regulated by some system of authority: the symphony conductor demands a particular passage be emphasized; the umpire determines when a baseball game is rained out; the shopkeeper decides how many hours employees must work. The family and classroom in particular are bound by this reality. Someone needs to lead these groups as they experience the daily events of home and school.

The authority inherent in the adult-child relationship cannot be avoided because adults know all kinds of things that children have yet to learn and have yet to develop the skills to understand. When we choose to act on our knowledge by controlling, encouraging, or restraining children's behavior, we are doing so in their behalf. To deny children this direction and guidance because they may resent it or because we think they can always learn from their mistakes is foolhardy. The notion that children ultimately know what's best for them has to be viewed with considerable caution. Among other things, children don't always know what foods are best for them or that it takes hard work to learn.

Because they lack adult experience and knowledge, children must be taught a responsible approach to themselves and to others. We provide a model of how one can live responsibly in society, a model which is important even if children later reject it. They need something against which to test their own experience of life. Deciding what set of behaviors and values they wish to follow is incredibly difficult in the rapidly changing world in which we live today. Firm, stable viewpoints on the part of adults give children something either to depend upon or to rebel against. Most people, for example, would agree that it is no favor to expose children to different religions at an early age in order to help them decide later on in life which religion to adopt. While choice helps a child to grow up, it is also useful to consider how restriction can enhance a child's growth as well.

Even when we realize that the judicious exercise of authority is not damaging, it is difficult to feel comfortable about setting limits, directing children's actions, or determining when they are able to make their own decisions. The standards of today are different from our childhood and change from year to year for adults also. There are so many varying and contradictory opinions about what is the best way to parent or teach that we simply may not know which advice to choose.

Furthermore, children expect more freedom than ever before. They live in a highly youth-oriented culture which stresses not only their right to live without the restrictions of past genera tions, but also encourages them to believe that they know today's "scene" better than we do. As a result, many adult beliefs and actions get tested against the "wisdom" of children's peers, TV shows, commercial messages, or other fashionable sources of knowledge.

Finally, it must be pointed out that not only do children expect more freedom but adults do too. We are part of what has been labeled the "me generation." Doing your own thing has become an expectation for almost every adult. It has also added to the dilemma of adult authority. Are we hypocritical to want to live our own life and yet direct and guide the lives of our children?

It is no wonder that we are confused and unable to act decisively with children. With so little support to assume authority, we can easily get discouraged and feel like mere bystanders in children's lives. We may watch children do poorly at school, date at age eleven, or stay up too late—all with a sense of frustration. We hope for the best but too often we feel stripped of any real power to influence children's physical, emotional, and intellectual well being.

As if this lack of support were not enough, our society sets before us an array of ideals that muddy the waters even further. These are ideals of what a parent or teacher *should* be like. They are so deeply embedded in our culture that we may be unaware

how extensively they shape our behavior. The following are some
of the more insidious and, in many ways, damaging ideals.

The Ideal of Perfection

The notion that parents and teachers are expected to handle
every situation in the best possible way is the overriding societal
ideal from which all others follow. Superlatives, in our country,
are everywhere. We are told about the perfect cleanser, the
whiter than white bleach, the ultimate life-style. It is no wonder
that we fall prey to the ideal of perfection. If everything from shirt
collars to toilet bowls must be dealt with perfectly, then surely
children must be raised perfectly.

Underlying most ideals is a myth. More simply put, there is an
assumption which supports the ideal but has little or no basis in
fact. The myth that encourages adults to accept perfection as
their goal is that children can be seriously damaged if an adult
makes one false move. Parents have been told that the psychological health of their children is totally determined by the way they
deal with them. Teachers have been told that they hold the key
not only to the learning of academic skills, but also to students'
self-esteem.

To believe that children will be damaged because we make lots
of mistakes or because we too can be selfish, irritable, or pig-
headed is unfounded. Even if our actions set back a child, they are
unlikely to leave permanent scars. Children have a natural resili-
ency to aid them in dealing with our imperfections, and eventually, with their own.

The Ideal of the Omnipotent Provider

A direct outgrowth of the ideal of perfection is the unwarranted notion that adults can, and should, provide everything
children need; that it is our job to understand what they need,
not only this minute but every moment of every future day;
that we should be sure to purchase all the toys and gadgets
that promise rapid intellectual development; that we should always help them with their homework; and should give them
all the Band-Aids and hugs necessary to soothe even the most
minor distress.

Why should adults try so hard to be omnipotent providers? It seems we accept the myth that providing is more necessary than denying. No one approves of spoiling children but adults often assume that children are more needy than they really are. We overlook children's ability to cope with frustration and adapt to new situations, an ability they can use when adults refuse to do everything for them or give them everything they want.

The Ideal of Rationality

We may also assume adults are required to be consistently logical and rational in their interactions with children. Dealing with children is often frustrating and arouses strong emotions. Yet the belief persists that we must be objective and rational at all times—that unless we tightly control our emotions, we will frighten or harm children with our anger, fear, or impatience. By holding in our emotions, however, the feelings often accumulate and when we do lose control, it is way out of proportion to the situation.

We know that people are not always rational and that sometimes the world is crazy, erratic, and unfair. Children have a right to know this, too. Being exposed to adults who believe in the right to express feelings, even irrational ones, provides the child with a more realistic expectation of life. Presenting children with a rational, unemotional model to emulate may produce an overly controlled person who is unable to express either love or hate, joy or sadness.

The Ideal of Mastery

In order to be perfect, provide for all needs, and stay calm and rational, society says it is up to parents and teachers to learn appropriate skills and techniques. In part, effective parenting or teaching *is* dependent on a set of skills which can be learned. If we did not believe this, we would not be writing this book. But effectiveness also involves a less tangible but equally important component: trusting our own instincts. If we don't trust our own judgment, all the skills in the world will not help. Lack of self-trust will keep us from using whatever skills are suggested and render them useless. The fallacy lies in assuming that mastering techniques is the goal; in truth, mastery is secondary to self-confidence.

The Ideal of the All-Knowing Adult

Society also expects adults to know or find out the answers to every problem or conflict between adults and children. Because we are a technologically oriented people, we expect that experts have found or will find the answers to all our problems. Unfortunately, the problems inherent in human interaction cannot be solved as simply as problems in nonhuman areas; people change and their relationships change. Answers that made sense twenty years ago may not make sense today. What time should nine-year-olds go to bed? Should infants be fed on time schedules or on demand? When are children ready to read? How should students be graded?

We too often want and believe cut-and-dried answers to these kinds of questions. Although the wish to know what experts believe is good for the physical, psychological, and intellectual growth of children is understandable, there are very few clear answers to guide us. Instead, there are numerous opinions, some general and some specific, about how to deal with children.

No source, and certainly not this book, can provide all the information parents and teachers may believe they require to raise and teach children; so much depends on personal judgment and decision making.

The Ideal of the Lone Changer

In our society, a strongly held belief is that any individual can change the nature of his or her problems alone. Americans have always placed a high value on individual initiative and have held that a person should be able to pull himself up by his own bootstraps. We are prone not only to buy this idea but also to believe that seeking help when needed is a sign of weakness.

Consider the absurdity of this belief. Even the Lone Ranger, the epitome of individual ruggedness, has a friend, Tonto, to talk to and to depend on. Yet when we have a problem, we believe we should work it out alone.

In reality, our problems don't occur in a vacuum, but in a social system composed of other people. When we attempt to change the ways we deal with our children, they can either support or sabotage our efforts. The attitudes and actions of our spouses and colleagues also influence how well our attempts at change succeed.

The belief that we can change our lot without help or interference, that we operate in our own sphere without influences from others, is naïve. The people in our lives who are important to us will encourage or discourage our efforts at change. We need their assistance.

People typically respond to these ideals and underlying myths with *guilt*. They believe the ideal of perfection and see themselves as inadequate and inferior because they fall short of this goal. They are certain that by today's standards, they would be judged incompetent, ineffective, and irresponsible. This guilty verdict is so painful that inner responses to conflict with children become confused and the ability to act becomes frozen. As a result, they are unwilling to assume authority and to be in charge of children.

There *is* a more positive response to these societal ideals. We courageously reject the ideals which we have been taught and replace them with more realistic beliefs. If we can accept these alternative beliefs, it is much easier to be in charge of children. We assert that it's OK to make mistakes in dealing with children; we can trust ourselves to handle authority responsibly even if we're not sure of what the best "method" is in a given situation. There are no cut-and-dried answers to parenting and teaching and we should not consider it a sign of weakness to ask for help with our problems. We believe parents and teachers have a right to be emotional with children and that children can survive quite well even if we deny them many things they want.

ASSERTION AND CHILDREN

To convince ourselves that we have the right and responsibility to assume authority in our relations with children is an important first step. To be able to act on this belief, however, we need ways to express this confidence in our authority role. The premise of this book is that parents and teachers can convey such confidence through the use of *assertion*. Assertion encompasses a wide range of behaviors which strike a balance between passivity and aggression. Taken together, these behaviors provide a unique way to deal with children. Being assertive means that we don't always have to rant and rave to seek what we want nor must we give up out of fear of inviting anger or losing love. It also means that we don't have to do all the talking in a conflict or be the overly polite listener. Best of all, it means that we can take action without showing disrespect for children.

Assertion training has become one of the most widely sought experiences of the psychology world. People flock to assertion training groups in droves seeking to overcome social insecurity or to temper their anger. In large numbers, they have also been reading assertion books such as *Your Perfect Right* (Alberti and Emmons), *Don't Say Yes When You Want to Say No* (Fensterheim and Baer), and *When I Say No, I Feel Guilty* (Smith). A wish to be strong and yet responsible in interpersonal relationships is clearly evidenced by the popularity of assertion training.

What exactly is assertion? How is it different from nonassertion and aggression? We offer here some definitions given by Arthur J. Lange and Patricia Jakubowski in *Responsible Assertive Behavior* (1976):

> *Assertion* involves standing up for personal rights and express-ing thoughts, feelings, and beliefs in *direct, honest,* and *appro-priate* ways which do not violate another person's rights. The basic message in assertion is: This is what I think. This is what I feel. This is how I see the situation. This message expresses "who the person is" and is said without dominating, humiliat-ing, or degrading the other person.

> *Non-assertion* involves violating one's own rights by failing to express honest feelings, thoughts, and beliefs, and conse-quently permitting others to violate oneself, or expressing one's thoughts and feelings in such an apologetic, diffident, self-effac-ing matter that others can easily disregard them. . . . Non-assertion shows a lack of respect for one's own needs. It also sometimes shows a subtle lack of respect for the other person's ability to take disappointments, to shoulder some responsibil-ity, to handle his own problems, etc. The goal of non-assertion is to appease others and to avoid conflict at any cost.

> *Aggression* involves directly standing up for personal rights and expressing thoughts, feelings, and beliefs in a way which is often dishonest, usually inappropriate, and always violates the rights of the other person. . . . The usual goal of aggression is domination and winning, forcing the other person to lose. Winning is insured by humiliating, degrading, belittling, or

overpowering other people so that they become weaker and less able to express and defend their needs and rights. The basic message is: This is what I think—you're stupid for believing differently. This is what I want—what you want isn't important. This is what I feel—your feelings don't count.

To bring life to these terms, let's examine some assertive, nonassertive and aggressive behavior with children. Specifically, we will be concerned with a twelve-year-old girl, Sarah. If we were one of Sarah's parents, we could expect the following to happen:

It's 10:15 on a Wednesday night and Sarah is engrossed in a TV special. Ten o'clock is bedtime on school nights. By now, we've reminded her twice of the time but Sarah doesn't seem to have any intention of going to bed.

The scene now shifts to Sarah in school. If we were one of her teachers, the following might be taking place: Our sixth-grade class is discussing last night's homework assignment. As the discussion progresses, we realize that Sarah is unprepared for the third day in a row. We have discussed this with her on the two previous days but she is still unprepared today.

The examples that follow reflect only a few illustrations of how we might react nonassertively, aggressively, and assertively to Sarah's behavior. In reality, there are hundreds of variations of each kind of behavior.

Nonassertive Responses

I. Don is a good-hearted father. He wants to be a responsible parent and also wants his children to like and respect him. Avoiding conflict is one of his biggest needs. Because he dislikes arguments of any kind, Don might say for the third time:

Don: Sarah, it's time for bed.

Sarah: But Dad, I want to see the end of this show.

Don: When you don't do what we've agreed to, I feel awful. I'm only trying to do what's right. Kids *need* their sleep!

Sarah: Tomorrow's only a half day of school. Come on, Dad. I'll go to bed early tomorrow.

Don: But we've agreed that ten o'clock is bedtime.

Sarah: Just this once—please!

Don: I don't know what to do. I try so hard to be a good parent. (He leaves the room, throwing up his hands.)

II. Joan wants the children in her classroom to like her. She doesn't want to force them to learn, but she does get hurt when they don't recognize her kindly manner. She also hates to appear angry with her students.

> *Joan:* Sarah, I've tried to be nice about this but you're not prepared again today. What happened?
>
> *Sarah:* I lost my homework.
>
> *Joan:* Well, stay after class and we'll discuss it.
>
> *Sarah:* That's not fair. Tommy never does his homework and he doesn't have to stay after!
>
> *Joan:* All right. All right. But be prepared tomorrow.

Aggressive Responses

I. Alice values order and responsibility. She believes that rules are important and that it is the responsibility of parents to enforce them. But when rules are not followed, Alice feels that her authority is threatened and reacts with anger.

> *Alice:* Sarah, I've told you three times it's time for bed.
>
> *Sarah:* But, Ma, I just want to see the end of this show!
>
> *Alice:* Sarah, you're incredible. I tell you to go to bed and you just sit there. You never listen to anyone. No wonder you do so lousy in school! Who could learn anything when they're half asleep? Get upstairs. Right now!
>
> *Sarah:* But Ma, I want to watch this.
>
> *Alice:* I said now! I don't want to discuss it.
>
> *Sarah:* But Ma!
>
> *Alice:* One more word out of you and I'll. . . . (Sarah leaves the room quickly. She seems angry and hurt.)

II. Mike's rule of thumb is "never smile until Christmas." He believes that a class full of students can get out of hand if he seems too friendly. If children are to learn, Mike assumes the teacher must always have the upper hand.

> *Mike:* Sarah, you're really getting out of hand. This is the third day that you haven't done your homework. What do you think I should do with you?
>
> *Sarah:* I don't know.

Mike: What do you think, class? (The class remains silent.) Sarah, your parents and I are so disappointed in you. You've got so much potential but you'll never amount to anything unless you apply yourself!

Sarah: Yes, sir.

Mike: You'll stay after class today and complete your work. Also, I'm going to call your parents. Maybe together we will straighten you out.

Assertive Responses

I. Ben is not so different a parent from Don and Alice in that he, too, wants to be responsible and fair in his dealings with children. He is also concerned with being respected by his children and equally concerned with being respectful of them. He knows that goal requires both warmth and firmness.

Ben: Sarah, it's ten fifteen. We agreed that you'd go to bed at ten. I'd like you to go to bed now.

Sarah: But Dad, I want to see the end of this show

Ben: I know how you feel, honey. It's hard to have to leave something in the middle but I'd like you to go to bed now.

Sarah: You let Jimmy stay up late.

Ben: That's true. Sometimes I do let Jimmy stay up later.

Sarah: Five more minutes?

Ben: I know you'd like to stay up a few more minutes but it's time for bed. You're to go to bed now.

II. Rosemary knows that students need limits but she also realizes that ridicule or name-calling won't help. She wants to be fair with her students and tries hard to be a good role model.

Rosemary: Sarah, can I see you for a minute after class?

Sarah: Yes, Mrs. Stanley.

Later—

Rosemary: Sarah, your homework hasn't been done for three days. I want you to do it. Can we work out a plan to make sure it gets done?

Sarah: I don't know, maybe.

Rosemary: What happened last night?

Sarah: Well, I forgot to do it when I got home. Then, just when I was going to start it, my mother made me go to bed.

Rosemary: So it seems that the best plan might be to do your homework before dinner.

Sarah: I guess so.

Rosemary: What could you do to remind yourself to do it right away?

Sarah: Well, I guess I could put a note on my mirror.

Rosemary: That sounds like a good idea. Try that tonight and let me know first thing in the morning if the plan works.

Sarah: OK.

Rosemary: Good. I'll see you first thing in the morning.

These illustrations suggest widely discrepant responses to Sarah. They emerge from radically different approaches to the adult authority role.

The nonassertive parent and teacher (Don and Joan) want Sarah to go to bed and do her homework but concerns over the unpleasantness of a conflict with Sarah prevent them from taking a strong position. We can say, in effect, that the desire to be in charge is there but the willingness is not, so appeasement is chosen over confrontation.

The aggressive parent and teacher (Alice and Mike) seem loud and clear about who's in command. In reality, though, Alice and Mike may be reluctant bosses. By wanting all the power but none of its costs, they assume authority, but not willingly. The key is their need to intimidate Sarah. They convey an annoyance not only with Sarah's behavior but also with having to deal with the tension and conflict generated by Sarah's behavior. The intimidation says: "I am thoroughly uncomfortable with the fact that you don't see things my way and I want to make sure that you are so upset by my actions that I'll never have to get this angry again."

By contrast, the assertive parent and teacher (Ben and Rosemary) accept the tension created by Sarah. They realize that Sarah may not value the same things as they do. They know, as a friend of ours recently said, "Nothing's easy with kids." And yet, Ben and Rosemary are willing to be in charge. We say "willing" because they are also accepting responsibility for their decision. They know that although Sarah might be displeased, she need not be shamed or bullied. They are conveying to Sarah: "Our decision affects you and we will help you to accept it as best you can. We are also prepared to stand by it even if it is unpopular."

When we try to assert ourselves with other adults (a friend, a spouse, a supervisor), we can expect them to have roughly the same skills and understandings that we have. This expectation does not guarantee that we will get a positive response to what we want, but at least we have a fighting chance. For the same reason, we can be open to their assertions. With children, we can easily be frustrated from the start because children may have a difficult time seeing our point of view and difficulty expressing their own point of view.

Typically, assertions can be more matter of fact with adults than with children. Because of children's dependence and their sense of smallness in relationship to us, we often must temper our assertions to avoid frightening them. Our firmness must be softened with tenderness. Other times, we must be exceedingly forceful with our assertions because children can be more stubborn than adults and more determined to get their way. When children proclaim, "I don't want to!" or plead, "Can I have . . . ?", they usually do so with an assertiveness that most adults would envy.

Moreover, if an attempt to assert our rights with other adults fails, we have the option of leaving the relationship. Instead of working things out with coworkers, sales personnel, friends, or even a spouse, we can change jobs, shop elsewhere, find new friends, or get a divorce. Not so with children. In assuming the responsibility to care for them, we can't abandon children. They are dependent on adults for their sustenance, learning, and growth. Once this responsibility is accepted, we give up the right to leave them if things aren't going well.

Finally, we need to recognize that when parents and teachers assume the responsibility of caring for children, they are interested in standing up not only for their own rights and needs, but also for the rights and needs of the children for whom they are responsible. One consequence of the decision to parent or to teach is that adults occasionally have to put aside their own needs for the benefit of the child. In adult-to-adult relationships, there is less obligation to put aside one's own needs for the sake of someone else. Furthermore, in order to serve the best interests of children, adults must also make several decisions for them and enforce these decisions in rather strong ways. When adults choose such a role, they often feel unappreciated because some of their decisions and methods of enforcement will be unpopular. They may also feel anxious and guilty about asserting themselves because they are not certain what decisions and methods are the "right" ones.

Because of the complexity of adult-child relationships, some modifications and extensions to the assertion literature are necessary to provide the special guidance that parents and teachers need. That is the goal of this book.

One comment: The use of assertion with children is *not* an assortment of tactics to condition children's behavior nor is it some guaranteed plan to emerge satisfied (or victorious) from every conflict. The use of assertion is simply an honest, non-manipulative effort on the part of an adult to provide guidance and direction. By being assertive with children, we will be able to feel good about our authority role. And best of all, our children will respond to us because we convey a sense that we are in charge of ourselves and of them.

2 | The Necessity of Assertive Adult Authority

Why did the kids pour jam on the cat—
Raspberry jam all over the cat?
They did it cause we said 'no'!

Your daughter brings a young man in,
Says do you like him, pa?
Just say that he's a fool
And then you've got a son-in-law.

These lyrics from a song* in the play *The Fantastiks* illustrate with their wry humor the essential dilemma of assuming authority over children. Adults take a stand about what's best for children—but children are quite likely to disagree.

How are we to understand the nature of adult-child relationships? And how can we feel secure about asserting our authority? Why not avoid the problem of raspberry jam and foolish young men by staying out of children's lives as much as possible?

---

*"Never Say No" by Tom Jones and Harvey Schmidt

CONFLICT BETWEEN ADULTS AND CHILDREN EXISTS IN EVERY FAMILY AND CLASSROOM

Adults and children have different perspectives on almost everything: bedtimes, school achievement, TV, neatness, etc. A major reason for these varying perspectives has to do with the fact that children are not able to understand the world in the same way as adults. As children grow, so does their ability to understand events in more complex and generalized ways. In early childhood, however, thought is quite *egocentric* and children tend to act impulsively on their wishes. To be egocentric means to be more concerned with one's own wants and needs than with the wants and needs of others. This does not mean that young children are selfish or bad, but rather that they lack the ability to see things as part of a larger scheme. As children mature, their egocentricity and impulsivity decrease. This is a long process, however, extending into adolescence.

Given their egocentricity, children place a high value on exploration, fun, excitement, and simply doing what they want to do. This is as it should be because these values help them to learn, to attract people, and to risk new things. Adults, on the other hand, have the responsibility to guide and care for their inexperienced, egocentric charges. Their job is to oversee the physical and psychological development of children by providing them with love, safeguards for their health, and limits for their impulsive behavior. Therefore, parents and teachers value such things as carefulness and restraint. These opposing sets of values create conflict in every family and classroom.

Beyond these simple yet profound differences in their approach to life, adults and children view differently the *interrelationships* among members of a family or classroom. Children, understandably, cannot often see beyond their own immediate needs, wants, and surroundings. So it's natural that they have trouble appreciating all the ways in which their actions affect others and other people's actions affect them. The ability to put oneself in another's shoes or to understand the viewpoint of others develops slowly and children's success with understanding interrelationships is not complete until well into adolescence.

For example, your son may believe that thirty minutes is enough time for him to get ready for school in the morning. It could be possible that he can get up, get dressed, brush his teeth, make his bed, eat breakfast, make his lunch, gather his school books and permission slips, and put on his coat in a half an hour. But what if someone was using the bathroom when he needed it, or a parent was detained by a phone call and couldn't have breakfast ready on time, or the child was needed to clean up a mess that the dog made, or any number of things that could happen to upset this thirty-minute plan? A classroom also presents problems of interrelationships. For example, students may not see that a clean room requires considerable coordination and division of labor rather than merely keeping one's own desk tidy. Such interdependence is much better understood by adults. So they have a different idea as to how families and classroom groups as interrelated systems get ready for work or school, and do many other tasks. These opposing perceptions create conflict.

CONFLICTS BETWEEN ADULTS AND CHILDREN ARE NORMAL, NATURAL, AND NECESSARY

Imagine that we could live our entire lives expressing the values and fancies of children. Ah, what a lovely dream of spontaneity, pleasure, and freedom! No doubt we would learn and do some beautiful and important things in such an environment, but the planet Earth is a different place, with different realities. If we avoid conflict with children by indulging their impulses, they do not learn to cope with the realities of life, and their egocentric dream of self-fulfillment turns into a nightmare of dependence.

The job of children, after all, is to become increasingly independent of adults. To achieve this, children must do something incredibly difficult: They must figure out how to profit from adult wisdom *and* how to periodically challenge adult authority. If we don't provide the wisdom to profit from and don't establish the authority to be challenged, there is nothing to which children can react. Salvador Minuchin, a highly esteemed family therapist, puts the necessity for conflict this way:

Parents [we can add teachers] cannot protect and guide without at the same time controlling and restricting. Children cannot grow and become individuated without rejecting and attacking. The process of socialization is inherently conflictual.*

The assumption that conflict is important in the adult-child relationship is buttressed by years of research on the learning process. There is overwhelming evidence that a moderate amount of tension helps learning to occur. If we have no anxiety or tension about a learning situation, we will have little motivation to expend the energy necessary to master the situation. If we are extremely anxious about the situation, however, learning and performance will be inhibited.

When parents or teachers act nonassertively with children, they remove the need for learning. For example, if an adult gives in to a child's request to be dressed, it will take less time than if the child dressed himself. There is also a greater likelihood that the child's appearance will be neat and pleasant. But doing it for the child eliminates the need for the child to learn. Dressing a child is appropriate at an early age, but as the child matures and becomes capable of dressing himself, the adult can teach the skill and then expect the child to gradually take on this responsibility. Of course, this expectation will create tension in the relationship. Giving over responsibility to the child will increase dressing time, often result in strange color combinations, and can produce a cranky child and disappointed parent. The parent has to resist urges to "help."

Teachers are also faced with this decision. Children may ask for help with school work that the teacher knows they are capable of doing on their own. If the teacher does the work for them, the probability is high that the children won't learn the material.

This tension exists even into adolescence. If money is readily available to an adolescent, there is neither reason nor motivation for the youngster to seek a summer or part-time job. By eliminating the need to earn money, a parent may deprive the adolescent of valuable learnings that are derived from work experience.

Children learn little when adults are reluctant to push or challenge them, and become insecure when adults fail to set reasonable limits on their behavior. For example, a massive study of seventeen hundred fifth- and sixth-grade children undertaken by

*Salvador Minuchin, *Families and Family Therapy,* (Cambridge: Harvard University Press, 1974), p. 58.

Stanley Coopersmith* found that low self-esteem and poor adjustment to school can be directly related to nonassertive parenting. The key to understanding this relationship is the fact that nonassertive adults often have strong feelings about children's actions or requests, but are fearful of *acting* on these feelings. Consequently, when children test adult authority they cannot find clear limits. Left to their own devices, children will probably do what they want, but with a nagging sense of the adult's displeasure.

Over a period of time, the failure of the adult to communicate expectations causes tremendous pressure on children. They must weigh continually how to stay children and yet make all the behavioral decisions that the adult is abdicating. All this time, children suspect that there really are limits in the mind of the adult. They respond to their suspicions in two different ways. One way is to play things safe and be cautious around the adult. Children might be secretive about doing the things they really want to do; they might decide not to do or ask for something, trying to make their best guess as to how to stay on the adult's good side. Another way is to take what they can get, deflecting or absorbing whatever disguised adult rejection comes their way. It means outwitting, out-arguing, and outlasting the adult (except that the battle lines are not clearly drawn).

Either response, passive or active, requires a considerable amount of energy from a child. It is energy which is badly needed for all the positive tasks of learning and development. It is little wonder that children, so preoccupied, develop low self-esteem and have trouble in school.

Aggressive adults, by their rigidity and their burdensome demands, also inhibit learning and the development of self-esteem. Insisting that a three-year-old keep totally quiet in church, demanding "A" work in all subjects in school from a ten-year-old, and expecting adult decisions from a twelve-year-old can all be ways to discourage children. As with nonassertive adults, aggressive adults also avoid meaningful conflict with children, not by indulgence, but by expecting unquestioned obedience. Moreover, the children are no more secure. While they may know exactly what is expected of them, children of aggressive parents or teachers lack a feeling of mutuality in their relationships with adults.

*Stanley Coopersmith, *The Antecedents of Self-Esteem.* (San Francisco: W. H. Freeman and Co., 1967).

There is little dialogue between them and these children are unaware that adults appreciate their needs and capabilities.

Mutuality is especially important when children enter adolescence. Within reasonable limits, adults need to tell adolescents not only what they want and why, but also to allow adolescents to influence their judgment if there is disagreement. This possibility does not exist when adults are absolute in their demands and expectations.

The essence of parenting and teaching is the inevitability of conflict and tension. Whenever we fail to accept this state of affairs, whether by acquiescence or heavyhandedness, we may breed our own resentments toward children, inhibit their learning, and leave them insecure and angry.

ALL ADULTS HAVE POWER OVER CHILDREN

Although we sometimes feel that we are powerless in the face of children's defiance, we aren't; and if we try not to appear powerful with children, we can't. We are usually bigger and stronger than children. We also have control over the resources necessary for their survival—food, love, knowledge, rewards. Whether or not we believe it or like it, we have power over children.

In conflict situations, it is true that children have considerable leverage because they don't play by the same rules of social persuasion that adults do with each other. Children are simply more stubborn and less guilt-ridden than adults. But if they choose to, adults can take authoritative action when children's behavior needs to be controlled or restricted. What usually stops us from taking action is our own resistance. We assume too often that a catastrophe will occur if children are told no when they are hoping for yes or if penalties are imposed for serious misbehavior.

We once observed a single-parent mother who let her sixteen-year-old son leave the house any time, day or night. She failed to stop him, fearing that he would leave home permanently if she took strong measures to prevent his sudden departures. When she gained enough support from family therapy to take action (in her case, it was necessary to drag him back into the house), her entire self-image as a parent changed and her son's respect for her dramatically increased. To be sure, the mother took a risk since her son might instead have left home for good. But, more often than not, children appreciate powerful adults. They sometimes want to be told no or told what to do in a situation where their impulses tell them one thing and their fragile sense of self tells them another. *When adults are not strong for children, children feel compelled to supply their own strength.* Unfortunately, it comes out in the forms of violent temper tantrums or wanton disregard for adult wishes.

As much as we like to think that a family or classroom functions as a democracy, children correctly perceive that there is a power hierarchy to which they must ultimately accommodate themselves. We merely confuse children when we appear to be one of the gang. All adults must resort to power of some kind to handle the inevitable conflicts which emerge with children. Our values are so different that we are bound to be disappointed with many of the choices children make. When we try to work out our differences through democratic discussion, we can get very frustrated because a child's outlook is often irrational to the adult mind. Although children become more reasonable as they grow older, problems can not always be solved reasonably. The final authority of adults is often necessary.

THE WAY ADULTS EXPRESS THEIR POWER OVER CHILDREN CAN BE HARMFUL

It's not so much whether we use our power but how we do so that affects children's well-being. There are two ways, in particular, in which adults express their power over children that can have harmful effects on both the children and adults involved.

Intimidation

One harmful expression of adult power is *intimidation*. In this way of relating to children, we attempt to frighten a child into doing our will. The interaction becomes a power struggle, but we have the edge because of our experience. The following statements are examples of intimidation in action.

- "You're gonna get it if you don't do what I say."
- "Do it, or you'll wish you'd never been born."
- "I'm bigger than you, you know."

- "You know what happens to children who get sent to the Vice Principal's office."
- "You'll learn this if we have to stay here all night."

All of the statements imply a threat to the child's safety and/or self-esteem. The amount of tension created by intimidation is extreme and may either inhibit learning or produce learning that we didn't intend.

Children have minimal choices in response to this assault. They may become submissive and do our bidding. Or they may become passive-aggressive; children may seemingly do our bidding but attempt to retaliate in other ways (failing at school, being inept, etc.). In either case, children still learn to be *just like us*. Perhaps not to us but to others. An extreme example of this is the abused child who becomes a child abuser as an adult. Research on aggression, especially the work of social learning psychologist Albert Bandura, gives unequivocal support to the fact that aggressive adult models not only teach children how to be aggressive, but also reduce children's inhibitions against acting aggressively.*

Parents and teachers who resort to using intimidation often do so in an attempt to reduce the frustration that they feel. Very few adults are always intimidating, but many adults who have tried other approaches conclude that the only language children understand is intimidation. Although they may not like being so tough, they feel it's the only way to get through to children and coerce them into behaving, at least for a while. So periodically, the adult becomes aggressive, goes on the rampage, and the children fall in line. But compliance only lasts for a time and another outburst becomes necessary. A vicious cycle has been established, and unfortunately, the children and the adults are teaching each other to behave in ways that neither likes.

Guilt

The other harmful way to express power over children is to induce guilt. Power through guilt is less obvious than power through intimidation because it feels more kindly. Because of our

*Albert Bandura, *Aggression: A Social Learning Analysis.* (Englewood Cliffs: Prentice-Hall, Inc., 1973).

own guilt about being authority figures, we disguise an attempt to produce the behavior we desire from children by making them feel guilty as well.

The following examples may help to clarify what we mean.

- "What will your mother think?"
- "I sat up until two o'clock waiting for you."
- "Your brother always did so well in school."
- "I don't know where I went wrong."
- "I've done everything possible to be nice to you today."
- "Your parents will be so disappointed with this grade."
- "I'm going crazy; I can't stand it anymore."
- "Your father needs peace and quiet when he comes home from work."
- "I try so hard to keep this house neat."

Guilt-inducing statements tend to be indirect. Instead of directly requesting a behavior (for example, come in on time, clean your room, etc.), the parent or teacher indirectly addresses the issue, abdicating responsibility for the request. The effect on the child is a feeling of guilt for letting down the adult.

We may not be aware of the manipulative quality of these kinds of statements; children will often do what we want them to do without our taking any direct responsibility for our demands. And because we are not directly demanding anything, we don't have to worry about being seen as autocrats. Moreover, we often avoid conflict. If we don't directly demand something, how can children be upset with us? The use of guilt is a subtle but very powerful method of getting our way.

When confronted with guilt-inducing statements, children can become very frustrated: It's hard to be angry with someone you've supposedly hurt, and it's hard to say no to an unspoken request. If children don't comply, they may feel even more guilty for causing pain to someone they love.

Yes, the inducement of guilt often produces the desired behavior, but what do children learn from such interactions? We believe they learn the negative patterns of being indirect when talking to others, and of never confronting others directly with feelings or requests. They also internalize these guilt feelings, and question their sense of self. By disappointing people, they begin to see themselves as unworthy. And as Erik Erikson has vividly depicted in his writings on human development, too much shaming may not lead to genuine obedience but to a secret desire to get away with things unseen.*

ADULT POWER CAN BE USED RESPONSIBLY

Some psychologists and educators believe that any direct use of power (no matter how it is expressed) destroys our relationship with children and should be avoided at all costs. Instead, they urge parents and teachers to depend on active communication and mutual problem solving to handle conflict and misbehavior. We disagree. As we have noted, children rely on our power to set rules and guide them. Power which respects children's feelings and is sensitive to their learning capacities does not destroy relationships. Adult power can be used indiscriminately and in desperation, but it can also be used responsibly.

The major research support for our position comes from the widely acclaimed studies of Diana Baumrind, a noted developmental psychologist.† Baumrind has found that adults who balance warmth with high control, and high demands with clear communication about what is required of a child, enjoy little discord or dissension in their homes or classrooms (although spirited conflict may arise at times). Children under the care of such adults are also more self-controlled, friendly, and assertive than children under authoritarian or permissive control.

The responsible use of adult power is demanding. We need to accept the inevitability of conflict with children and commit ourselves not to minimize or exacerbate the tension conflict brings. We also must be flexible, taking control when we think it is necessary and relinquishing control as a child becomes competent to assume a particular responsibility.

We will use the term *assertive adult authority* to describe the responsible use of adult power (since it requires us to express

*Erik Erikson, *Childhood and Society.* (New York: W. W. Norton, 1950.)
†See, for example, D. Baumrind, "Authoritarian vs. Authoritative Parental Control," *Adolescence,* 3 (1968): 256–261; and D. Baumrind, "Current Patterns of Parental Authority," *Developmental Psychology Monographs* 1971, 1:1–103.

ourselves through assertion rather than guilt or intimidation). Examples of an assertive expression of adult authority are:

- "I realize that it's easier to play ball without a coat on, but because it's cold, I want you to wear your coat."
- "It's important to me that your work is finished by the end of the period."
- "I know you'd like to stay up later than nine o'clock but nine o'clock is your bedtime."
- "You and Jimmy are quarreling? What do you think you can do to set things right?"
- "I know that some parents allow their fourteen-year-olds to date but I want you to wait until you're fifteen."

Each of these statements reflects a simple, straightforward expression of what the adult questions, believes, or wants. When a position is taken, it is announced without excessive justification or other symptoms of defensiveness. Sensitivity to the child's feelings are conveyed instead. When a matter seems appropriate for a child's decision making, it is actively encouraged.

ASSERTIVE ADULT AUTHORITY INVOLVES PERSONAL JUDGMENT

Guilt and intimidation are practically automatic reflexes. We are so accustomed to expressing power over children in these ways that little thought is required. Assertive adult authority involves reflection about what we want and how we behave and consideration of the child's behavior, age, and situation. Through this introspection, we make choices about whether to act or not and, if we act, what methods to use. *Our decisions are personal ones; they cannot be made by others.*

The most important personal judgment we need to make is whether or not to assume responsibility in a given situation. Demanding things of children means that we accept the task of seeing matters through. Therefore, if we wish to assume responsibility in a situation, we must be willing to absorb children's displeasure with our demands without intimidating them, inducing guilt, or changing our minds out of fear of conflict. Giving responsibility over to children, on the other hand, means giving them real control over a matter. We can tell them our point of view but we must be willing to let children absorb the consequences of their own decisions.

Take, for example, the problem of the tidiness of a child's bedroom. If our best judgment is to insist that it be kept tidy, it is *our* responsibility to ensure that this is accomplished. We must risk being the villain, express our demand clearly and nondefensively, and persist with it until it is fulfilled. Above all else, we do not shame or bully children when they resist by saying, for example, "Cleaning your room is really your responsibility. I shouldn't have to keep after you like this." When we decide to give the responsibility over to our children, we can still express our *wish* for a tidy room and the reason for it, but it is then the children's right to respond to this wish as they see fit. If our wish is not fulfilled, we are acting irresponsibly by reverting to guilt or intimidation to control children's actions.

In situations where negotiation and compromise are possible and desirable, so-called *nonpower* approaches can be very useful. Probably the most well-known of these approaches is the "No-lose Method" advocated by Dr. Thomas Gordon in his books, *Parent Effectiveness Training, Teaching Effectiveness Training,* and *P.E.T. in Action.* The idea behind the method is to solve conflicts in such a way that the wishes of both adults and children are preserved as much as possible. The advantage of using this mutual problem solving approach is that children are less resentful; therefore, it encourages more lasting solutions to persistent conflicts.

Let's assume that a child does not want a haircut but his parents want him to have one. Instead of forcing the haircut on the child or letting the child have his way, both parties could examine solutions to their conflict in which neither feels that the other won. For example, the child might agree to the haircut if a hair stylist could be found who can minimize the effect of shorn hair.

Our own experience suggests that nonpower approaches are valuable options for adult authority figures. They are, in effect, ways to give up our power when we feel we can risk a more open relationship. Such risk-taking by the adult is quite important in teaching children self-reliance. But *nonpower approaches still remain options, and not starting points.* Every family or classroom has to have a person in charge. What happens there is too complex and the conflict too frequent to always leave matters to mutual problem solving. Nonpower approaches are best suited for situations in which adults judge that negotiation and compromise are the ways to deal with a problem because in this approach it is of paramount importance that adults are willing to live with the agreed upon solution.

If assertive adult authority relies so much on personal judgment, how do we know *when* to control and *when* to let go? How do we know when a child can handle a task? How do we know when a child is not ready to do what we are requesting?

Common sense dictates that we impose direction when, in our best judgment, that direction teaches the child something important, and/or is necessary for the well-being of the family or classroom. For example, a nine-year-old might not want to take a bath or shower daily or even weekly, yet a parent may judge that the shower or bath is required both for what it teaches about personal cleanliness and for the benefit of the health and sensitivities of other family members. A young student may not see the value of learning to multiply (adding may seem just as easy), but a teacher may insist, knowing that multiplication is a real time saver when math problems get more difficult.

But it's also common sense to postpone our request when the child is not physically able to accomplish the task, is not psychologically ready for it, or is already overloaded with demands. For example, if a young child lacks the perceptual motor coordination to learn cursive writing or the maturity to care for a dog, it would be unwise to expect the child to do these things. Likewise, we would not insist on music lessons for a child who is already involved in three extracurricular activities in school.

The reality is that no magical formulas exist to determine the readiness of a child to perform a specific task. Children mature, physically and psychologically, at different rates. The fact that other children of a particular age are able to perform a certain task does not necessarily mean that a child or student in our care is ready. These decisions call for your best judgments. Obviously, if a child seems particularly behind his or her age group in a given area, we should consider seeking an expert opinion. In general, our powers of observation and knowledge of this particular child will help us decide. Our judgments, however, should not depend solely on a child's resistance to a particular task; don't assume that if the child balks, he's not ready. To guide children often means to endure their resistance.

Given the degree of personal judgment required by an assertive authority role, it is awfully tempting to rely instead on intimidation and guilt when children disagree with us. As we discussed in chapter 1, being assertive with children also means being honest and direct about what you want and respecting children's natural uneasiness with being given an order, guideline, or refusal. It means, among other things, dealing with children issue-by-issue instead of lumping together all their misbehaviors. It means showing interest in their side of the argument and finding ways to make our demands more attractive to the children. Finally, it means accepting a child's anger and resentment while sticking to an unpopular stand.

None of us can consistently be assertive with children. We will continue to find ourselves in situations where the pressure of the moment causes us to resort to intimidation or guilt. But by using assertive adult authority as our overall approach to parenting and teaching, we will be able to express our best judgments about what is good for children and have our opinions respected by them.

This book contains various ideas and strategies that people have found useful in building and maintaining a responsible, assertive approach to dealing with children. Our experience in working with teachers and parents has taught us that the recipe for building and maintaining an assertive authority role has different ingredients for different people. For some adults, re-evaluating their beliefs about adult-child relationships has been the key ingredient. For others, learning new skills made the difference.

Because the recipe for assertive adult authority depends on the individual parent or teacher, we will attend to all the ingredients that have been useful to the wide range of parents and teachers with whom we have worked. These ingredients include looking at the following:

- influences on our authority style
- the way we present ourself to children through words and actions
- the strategies we've developed to prevent excessive conflict
- the range of techniques we have to deal with conflicts when they arise

- the way we understand and respond to the developmental struggles children experience
- the kind of relationship and involvement we have with children
- the way we relate to and gain support from the other adults in our environment
- the way we deal with our own resistance to change

Take what you need. One or more of these areas may provide the key ingredient for you.

3 | Looking at Your Authority Style

There is an often-told joke that nervous breakdowns are hereditary; they come from our children! Because of the frustrations we suffer in guiding them, there is an understandable wish to consider children to be the source of all our troubles. But as adults, we can aggravate or ameliorate our difficulties and frustrations by our treatment of children—by the stances all of us take as people in charge of families or classrooms.

Let's call these stances we take our *authority style*. Authority style encompasses many dimensions: how active or passive, how hostile or accepting, how clear or ambiguous, and how controlling or permissive we are. It is the behavioral expression of our attitudes toward self, toward our authority role, and toward children all wrapped together. None of us has a totally consistent style, but we tend to repeat the same behavior in certain situations, and our children take note. They do not describe the patterns in our behavior with words like assertive, aggressive, or nonassertive, but they undeniably recognize differences in the way we act out our authority roles. Their responses are as different as our presentations: To some, they respond with fearful obedience; to others, they give lip service; to still others, they are accepting.

Our hope is that you will get a clearer reading on your authority style and its effect on children by going through three activities which follow.

ACTIVITY I: WHEN IS YOUR AUTHORITY STYLE ASSERTIVE?

As a way to begin, we would like you to fill out an assertiveness inventory (there is a form for parents and a form for teachers). The first part of the inventory asks you to identify how you are most likely to respond to common situations in the life of a parent or teacher. The second part requires you to agree or disagree with some statements about yourself.

The Parent Assertiveness Inventory

PART I

INSTRUCTIONS

Below are ten situations that occur in the lives of parents. None of them suggests a definite age for the children so that you might be better able to imagine the situations happening to you. There are numerous ways a parent might act or react in each situation. We have included three possible responses for each situation. Choose one which best predicts how you would behave. Be careful to select the response which comes closest to *how you would most likely act in the situation,* not how you would prefer to act. If none of the choices provided captures how you are most likely to act, put your prediction in your own words.

1. ALTHOUGH YOU HAVE REPEATEDLY ASKED YOUR CHILD TO CLEAN UP HER ROOM, SHE KEEPS POSTPONING THE CLEANUP BY SAYING, "I'LL DO IT LATER."

   In this situation, I'm most likely to:
   a. lose my patience and tell off my child *
   b. leave my child alone or clean the room myself
   c. persist with the request until it is done *

2. YOUR CHILD IS CONTINUALLY CRYING FOR THINGS HE IS CAPABLE OF ASKING FOR WITH WORDS. HE IS RESTED AND IN GOOD HEALTH. YOU HAVE ALREADY EXPLAINED THE NEED FOR USING WORDS.

   In this situation, I'm most likely to:
   a. ignore the crying even if I have to leave the room *

b. spank my child in complete frustration

c. break down and give in to what he wants

3. YOUR CHILD COMES TO YOU WITH A BOOK IN HAND JUST AS YOU ARE SETTLING DOWN TO SOME PRIVATE TIME FOR YOURSELF. SHE WANTS YOU TO READ TO HER. IT'S BEEN A FEW DAYS SINCE THE CHILD LAST MADE THIS REQUEST, BUT YOU'RE NOT IN THE MOOD NOW TO SPEND TIME WITH HER.

In this situation, I'm most likely to:

a. read to her anyhow

b. refuse for now, but suggest another time

c. provide some excuse why I can't read to her

4. YOU HAVE DISCOVERED THAT YOUR CHILD HAS TAKEN $5 FROM YOUR WALLET WITHOUT YOUR PERMISSION AND HAS SPENT IT.

In this situation, I'm most likely to:

a. ask where I've gone wrong for him to do such a thing

b. ground him from leaving the house (except for school) for a month

c. express my anger and work out some arrangement for the money to be earned back

5. ONCE AGAIN, YOUR CHILD COMPLAINS THAT YOU HAVE STRICTER RULES AND REGULATIONS THAN THOSE OF ALL HER FRIENDS' PARENTS. TO YOU, THE COMPLAINT IS IRRELEVANT. YOU HAVE YOUR OWN RULES.

In this situation, I'm most likely to:

a. briefly repeat my views on the matter

b. tell my child that she is being ridiculous

c. feel badly and give in a little on my rules

6. YOU OBJECT TO YOUR CHILD'S DESIRE TO GO TO A VIOLENT MOVIE, BUT YOUR CHILD STRENUOUSLY ARGUES THAT VIOLENCE DOESN'T AFFECT HIM AS IT MAY OTHER KIDS.

In this situation, I'm most likely to:

a. try to out-argue my child

b. become confused about what to do

c. show respect for my child's point of view but hold fast to my objection

7. TO AVOID ANOTHER BITTER FEUD WITH YOUR CHILD, YOU GRACIOUSLY GIVE IN TO A REQUEST WHICH YOU NORMALLY REFUSE. JUST ONE HOUR LATER, THE CHILD APPROACHES YOU AGAIN WITH ANOTHER REQUEST YOU USUALLY DON'T GRANT.

In this situation, I'm most likely to:

a. politely refuse

    b. blow up in anger

    c. accede to the request but for only "one more time"

8. YOUR CHILD ASKS YOU TO DRIVE HER TO A PARTY SEVERAL MILES FROM WHERE YOU LIVE. SHE WANTS TO GO BADLY. NO OTHER PARENT CAN TAKE YOUR CHILD BECAUSE THE OTHER KIDS INVITED TO THE PARTY LIVE ELSEWHERE. YOU HAVE BEEN FEELING TOO MUCH LIKE A CHAUFFEUR LATELY.

In this situation, I'm most likely to:

    a. complain that my child is only looking out for her needs

    b. refuse but try to make it up to my child somehow ♥

    c. explain how I'm feeling lately and say no

9. YOU HAVE BEEN MAKING A LOT OF STOPS TAKING CARE OF IMPORTANT ERRANDS. YOUR CHILD IS ALONG WITH YOU BUT IS GETTING IRRITABLE AND WANTS TO GO HOME. YOU DESPERATELY NEED TO COMPLETE YOUR ERRANDS.

In this situation, I'm most likely to:

    a. complain to my child how unreasonable she is

    b. beg my child to be patient a little longer ◆

    c. express empathy for my child's needs but also inform him that I will have to complete the errands

10. YOUR CHILD IS UNFRIENDLY WHEN YOUR (ADULT) FRIENDS VISIT. THEY TRY TO RELATE TO YOUR CHILD IN A PLEASANT MANNER BUT SHE GIVES THEM A COLD SHOULDER AND WALKS AWAY.

In this situation, I'm most likely to:

    a. let it be

    b. tell my child directly what I want from her

    c. accuse my child of being selfish and unfriendly ◆

PART II

INSTRUCTIONS

Below are twelve statements which may describe your behavior as a parent. If you strongly agree that a statement is true about you, check the space after YES. If you strongly disagree, check NO. If your response is not strong agreement or disagreement, choose one of the four middle categories.

1. I am unclear to my child(ren) about what I expect from them.
   NO!__ No__ No?__ Yes?_∙ Yes__ YES!__

2. When my child(ren)'s arguments are justified, I listen and acknowledge their valid points.
   NO!__ No__ No?_∙ Yes?__ Yes__ YES!__

3. I tend to dismiss the problems my child(ren) have.
   NO!__ No_•_ No?__ Yes?__ Yes__ YES!__
4. I let my child(ren) treat me like a butler or a maid.
   NO!__ No__ No?_•_ Yes?__ Yes__ YES!__
5. I worry that my child(ren) will disapprove of me.
   NO!__ No__ No?_‹_ Yes?_⁄_ Yes__ YES!__
6. Even if it takes a long time, I am persistent about asking for the behavior I want from my child(ren).
   NO!__ No__ No?__ Yes?__ Yes_•_ YES!__
7. I resort to tricking or out-smarting my child(ren) to get what I want.
   NO!_‹_ No__ No?__ Yes?__ Yes__ YES!__
8. I can accept my child(ren's) negative feelings toward me.
   NO!__ No__ No?_•_ Yes?__ Yes__ YES!__
9. I can withstand my child(ren's) maneuvers to get me to change an unpopular action or decision.
   NO!__ No__ No?__ Yes?__ Yes__ YES!_·_
10. I give in to my child(ren)'s requests hoping they will be nice to me in return.
    NO!_·_No__ No?__ Yes?__ Yes__ YES!__
11. When I'm angry with my child(ren), I can't help calling them names or saying nasty things.
    NO!_˙_No__ No?__ Yes?__ Yes__ YES!__
12. I nag.
    NO!__ No__ No?__ Yes?__ Yes_•_ YES!__

The Teacher Assertiveness Inventory

PART I

INSTRUCTIONS
Below are ten situations which occur in the lives of teachers. None of them suggests a definite age for the children so that you might be better able to imagine the situations happening to you. There are numerous ways a teacher might act or react in each situation. We have included three possible responses for each situation. Choose one which best predicts how you would behave. Be careful to select the response which comes closest to *how you would most likely act* in the situation, not how you would prefer to act. If none of the choices provided captures how you are most likely to act, put your prediction in your own words.

1. A PLEASANT BUT TERRIBLY DISORGANIZED STUDENT IN YOUR CLASS CAN SELDOM FIND HER BOOKS OR WORKSHEETS WHEN NEEDED. SHE COMES TO YOU WITH A LOOK OF FRUSTRATION AND REPORTS THAT SHE CAN'T LOCATE A BOOK REPORT DUE THAT DAY.

   In this situation, I'm most likely to:
   a. sternly lecture the student about the importance of keeping track of her things
   b. say nothing and look exasperated
   c. empathize with her frustration and insist on an agreement as to how this might be avoided in the future

2. A LARGE PART OF YOUR CLASS COMPLAINS THAT A TEST YOU GAVE WAS UNFAIR. IN YOUR ESTIMATION, THE TEST MAY HAVE BEEN HARDER THAN THE STUDENTS EXPECTED BUT IT WAS VALID AND COVERED EXACTLY THE MATERIAL PROMISED.

   In this situation, I'm most likely to:
   a. worry that my students will dislike me if I don't do something to make things up to them
   b. hold an open discussion of their complaints to be sure I haven't overlooked something
   c. try to destroy the logic of their arguments

3. CONFIDENT THAT HE HAS DONE A GOOD JOB, A STUDENT SHOWS YOU SOME WORK (e.g., A COMPOSITION, A REPORT, A DRAWING) HE HAS JUST FINISHED AND ASKS IF YOU LIKE IT. YOU DON'T LIKE IT, AND YOU FEEL THAT THE STUDENT COULD DO MUCH BETTER.

   In this situation, I'm most likely to:
   a. tease the student about the poor quality of the work
   b. somehow avoid saying anything about my opinion out of fear that I will upset the student
   c. reveal my honest feelings about the work and make suggestions for improvement

4. A STUDENT WANTS YOUR HELP AGAIN ON A DIFFICULT MATH WORKSHEET. YOU CAN APPRECIATE THE STUDENT'S NEED FOR SUPPORT BUT YOUR PATIENCE HAS WORN THIN.

   In this situation, I'm most likely to:
   a. act annoyed by the student's request so that I will be left alone
   b. provide some excuse why I can't help now
   c. honestly respond, "I'm not up to helping you now"

5. IT'S A WARM, NICE DAY AND YOUR STUDENTS BEG YOU TO HOLD CLASS OUTSIDE. YOU DON'T LIKE OUTDOOR CLASSES BECAUSE YOU FIND THAT THE STUDENTS' ATTENTION WANDERS.

In this situation, I'm most likely to:
a. express understanding of their wish but hold fast to my desire to stay indoors
b. accede to their wish
c. put down their request as an attempt to avoid work

6. A TIMID STUDENT CONTINUALLY FINDS EXCUSES TO AVOID MAKING SOCIAL CONTACT WITH OTHER STUDENTS. YOU BELIEVE THAT MORE RELATIONS WITH PEERS WILL HELP HER GREATLY.

In this situation, I'm most likely to:
a. warn the student that she will never have friends if the avoidance continues
b. leave the child alone for fear that I will upset her with my prodding
c. persistently encourage the child to play and work with other students

7. YOU HAVE PROMISED YOUR STUDENTS SOME FREE TIME AT THE END OF THE PERIOD OR DAY IF THEY GET ALL THEIR WORK DONE. WHEN THE TIME COMES, THEY HAVE CLEARLY NOT BEEN AS PRODUCTIVE AS YOU EXPECTED.

In this situation, I'm most likely to:
a. scold them concerning their lack of productivity
b. cancel the free time without much comment
c. let them have the free time anyhow, so you will not appear like a villain

8. UPON READING STUDENT ANSWERS TO THE ESSAY QUESTION TEST YOU GAVE THEM, YOU DISCOVER THAT THEY HAVE NOT DONE AS WELL AS YOU HAD EXPECTED. COMPARED TO OTHER CLASSES, VERY FEW STUDENTS WOULD GET EVEN A "B" GRADE.

In this situation, I'm most likely to:
a. give my usual quota of A's and B's out of concern for being perceived a tough teacher
b. grade them low and briefly express my disappointment over the class's performance when returning the tests
c. grade them low and go to great lengths to justify the grades given

9. YOU HAD PROMISED YOUR CLASS A MOVIE FOR TODAY'S LESSON, BUT YOU FORGOT TO PICK IT UP FROM THE DISTRIBUTOR ON THE WAY TO SCHOOL. YOUR STUDENTS WERE LOOKING FORWARD TO THE MOVIE.

In this situation, I'm most likely to:
a. apologize profusely and promise it won't happen again

    b. express short, honest comments of regret

    c. strongly defend my right to make a mistake once in a while

10. STUDENTS HAVE AGREED TO KEEP THEMSELVES QUIETLY OCCUPIED WHILE YOU GO ON AN ERRAND TO THE SCHOOL OFFICE. WHEN YOU RETURN, BEDLAM EXISTS IN THE CLASSROOM.

In this situation, I'm most likely to:

    a. convince myself that I should not have expected them to keep their agreement and drop the matter

    b. scream my head off

    c. take a privilege away from the class

PART II

INSTRUCTIONS

Below are twelve statements which may describe your behavior as a teacher. If you strongly agree that a statement is true about you, check the space after YES. If you strongly disagree, check NO. If your response is not strong agreement or disagreement, choose one of the four middle categories.

1. I am honest with all my students.
NO!__ No__ No?__ Yes?__ Yes__ YES!__

2. I put down the petty complaints my students have.
NO!__ No__ No?__ Yes?__ Yes__ YES!__

3. I try to avoid students who give me a hard time.
NO!__ No__ No?__ Yes?__ Yes__ YES!__

4. I act more than I talk.
NO!__ No__ No?__ Yes?__ Yes__ YES!__

5. I worry whether or not I'm popular with my students.
NO!__ No__ No?__ Yes?__ Yes__ YES!__

6. I can enforce decisions my students don't like.
NO!__ No__ No?__ Yes?__ Yes__ YES!__

7. I expect my students to know what I want without having to tell them.
NO!__ No__ No?__ Yes?__ Yes__ YES!__

8. Even if it takes a long time, I am persistent about asking for the behavior I want from my students.
NO!__ No__ No?__ Yes?__ Yes__ YES!__

9. I get into power struggles with difficult students.
NO!__ No__ No?__ Yes?__ Yes__ YES!__

10. I get flustered with students when I feel under pressure.
NO!__ No__ No?__ Yes?__ Yes__ YES!__

11. I can be nasty if the situation warrants it.
   NO!__ No__ No?__ Yes?__ Yes__ Yes!__
12. I'm too nice to my students.
   NO!__ No__ No?__ Yes?__ Yes__ YES!__

Interpreting Activity I

Look over your responses to the assertiveness inventory. You probably do not consistently respond one way, but when do certain behaviors repeat themselves? Do you find, for example, that you often accede when a child pushes you with a request? When are you clear? When do you have a need for control? When are you willing to communicate honestly? Do any patterns emerge?

The following key can be used in interpreting your responses. It indicates which behaviors for the situations in Part I are considered nonassertive, aggressive, and assertive; and which statements about yourself in Part II reflect nonassertive, aggressive, and assertive styles.

	Nonassertive Responses	Aggressive Responses	Assertive Responses
Part I (Parent)	1b; 2c; 3a; 4a; 5c; 6b; 7c; 8b; 9b; 10a	1a; 2b; 3c; 4b; 5b; 6a; 7b; 8a; 9a; 10c	1c; 2a; 3b; 4c; 5a; 6c; 7a; 8c; 9c; 10b
Part I (Teacher)	1b; 2a; 3b; 4b; 5b; 6b; 7c; 8a; 9a; 10a	1a; 2c; 3a; 4a; 5c; 6a; 7a; 8c; 9c; 10b	1c; 2b; 3c; 4c; 5a; 6c; 7b; 8b; 9b; 10c
	Nonassertive Statements	Aggressive Statements	Assertive Statements
Part II (Parent)	1; 4; 5; 10	3; 7; 11; 12	2; 6; 8; 9
Part II (Teacher)	3; 5; 10; 12	2; 7; 9; 11	1; 4; 6; 8

You can also find patterns in your responses by referring to the chart below. It identifies the kinds of responses used in the assertiveness inventory to depict nonassertive, aggressive, and assertive stances toward children.

NONASSERTIVE	AGGRESSIVE	ASSERTIVE
You:	You:	You:
are evasive	blow up in anger	persist
beg	get into power	listen to children's
act flustered	struggles	points of view
try to "make	endlessly argue	reveal honest
things do"	accuse	feelings
are confusing,	discredit children's	give brief
unclear	thinking	reasons
let yourself be	trick, tease, put	politely refuse
treated unfairly	down	to do something
worry about being	give harsh	empathize
popular	punishments	carry out reason-
are afraid of up-	nag	able consequences
setting children	withhold	make clear, di-
blame yourself	information	rect requests
	about what you	
	expect	

In our courses and workshops, we find that participants are sometimes anxious about whether they are nonassertive or aggressive or assertive in an absolute sense (as if these words described fixed, immutable traits). No one can categorically be labeled as such, as we act in all three ways at various times and in various combinations. Much can depend on the mood we are in, the child or group of children we are with, and the particular conflict we may be facing. Rather than choose a label for yourself, use this activity as a vehicle for becoming a better observer of yourself. Note what situations bring out different responses in you and select behaviors you would like to change.

There is also a dangerous tendency for people to think that assertive actions are always the right ones—as if it is never of value, to ourselves or to children, to blow up in anger or concede to a child's wish. Avoid self-castigation. Perhaps one of the most assertive actions you can take is to decide *not* to assert yourself all the time.

If you identify definite patterns in your responses to the inventory, you might find it useful to consider what self-image you are serving by acting out your authority in a certain way. Time and again we have found that adult behavior is influenced by these images—how adults *want* to appear to themselves and to children. Some adults worry that they are mean if they say no. Others may fret that they will seem pushy if they persist with their requests. Still others are afraid that they will be considered weak if they listen to a child's feelings. Is there a self-image you want to project that influences your actions as a parent or teacher?

ACTIVITY II: HOW HAS YOUR AUTHORITY STYLE BEEN INFLUENCED BY YOUR PARENTS?

This activity involves asking yourself how your authority style reflects the way your parents (and other significant people in your life) related to you as a child. Think for a moment (or discuss with a partner) how your parents would have responded to an assertiveness inventory. What were their patterns? How did they differ from each other, if at all, in authority style? And most important, what have you learned from each of them?

As an aid in this analysis, we have provided below a list of adjectives and phrases which might describe one or both of your parents. Circle those words which apply to your mother and place a rectangle around those which apply to your father. To compare yourself to each of your parents, check words and phrases which describe you.

manipulative	indirectly told you what she or he wanted	inconsistent
indecisive	firm	had many expectations
persistent	harsh	confusing, unclear
avoided conflict	easy to win over	temperamental
patient	protective	distant

Interpreting Activity II

Some years ago, there was an episode on the television program, "Rhoda," which humorously depicted how we model our parents' behavior. Rhoda disapproved of her sister (Brenda's) new boy-friend and lectured her about all his shortcomings. Brenda responded, "You know, you sound just like Ma." Taken aback by this remark, Rhoda reflected for a moment and then disclosed, "You know, you're right. Sometimes I wake up in the middle of the night from a dream that rollers are growing in my hair and I have an uncontrollable urge to vacuum."

Our behavior has indeed been shaped by our parents and other significant adults. But examining our parental models can be a two-edged sword. On one hand, such an analysis allows us to see in bolder relief our own patterns of behavior; we are then better able to identify aspects of our behavior we wish to enhance and aspects we wish to change. For example, if we notice the same indecisiveness in our parents as we sometimes see in ourselves, we might be encouraged to change the pattern. On the other hand, once we realize how long-standing any behavior pattern is, we might be discouraged from any real effort to change.

In our opinion, there is no easy way to resolve this dilemma. It is true that our early learning has an enormous impact on how we behave. But it is better to know what we are up against than pretend we can change any aspects of ourselves overnight. Let us imagine, for example, a person named Jim. His parents were, by and large, quite gentle. They never physically or verbally abused Jim. They were not persistent about what they wanted from Jim and gave in to many of his wishes. When Jim was young, his parents manipulated situations by tricking or bribing him. In the later years of Jim's childhood, they resorted to inducing feelings of guilt. For instance, they frequently hinted that Jim's lack of progress in school caused them to lose sleep. There is very little chance that Jim is now an assertive, honest, or firm parent or teacher because he simply has not been exposed to a model of assertion, honesty, and firmness. Our point is that Jim needs to recognize what his parents have taught him. He must realize that what he absorbed early in life has had a strong impact on his adult behavior. To make strides in a more assertive direction as a parent or teacher, Jim will have to confront the adult role model he has undoubtedly internalized with a great deal of courage and tenacity.

Examining your own parental models will raise many interesting possibilities. You may discover, for example, that you have learned different things from each of your parents. One may have taught you to be strict and tough-minded. The other parent may have taught you patience and understanding. Possibly you have learned to integrate the best of both parents into a coherent, effective authority style. Or you might notice that you imitate one parent in one kind of situation and imitate the other parent in another circumstance. Still another possibility is that you have adopted the opposite of your parents' style. Overall, this may have been very wise. But you may have rejected too quickly some of your parents' ways. If for example, your parents punished you a lot, and you have developed a style quite opposite to theirs, you may have rejected the firmness and strength which underscored your parents' punitiveness. While you may not wish to be punitive yourself, your parents still may have taught you something useful, something that Jim's parents didn't.*

Now is the time to reevaluate these past learnings. As children we had little choice. As adults, we can reflect on them and decide on new directions if desired.

ACTIVITY III: WHEN IS YOUR AUTHORITY STYLE EFFECTIVE?

In looking at your authority style, the bottom line is whether or not you get results. When do children respond to your requests? How much effort does it take? When are you able to say no to requests you can't meet or believe are unwise? How much respect do your refusals receive? The primary purpose of this final activity is to examine when you are effective at making decisions and enforcing your authority and when you are not.

First let's look at what demands you presently have for your children.

---

*Indeed, there has been considerable research indicating that adults who have rebelled against their parents' style seek to work out their rebellious feelings through their own children. Thus, if one's parents were very strict, the adult is likely to be permissive, not necessarily by preference, but for the purpose of getting back at one's parents.

Every child in your family or classroom is subject to a number of behaviors you expect him or her to do or not do. Some of these dos and don'ts are for all of the children; others might be reserved for a specific child. In the spaces provided below, write down all the important dos and don'ts that currently exist in your family or classroom. Include those for all the children as well as those for a specific child. Areas to consider are: assignments and chores, personal health and appearance, interpersonal relationships, safety, and the rights of others.

	Dos & Don'ts	Grade
1.		
2.		
3.		
4.		
5.		
6.		
7.		
8.		
9.		
10.		

Now give a grade for each item on your list. Here is the grading system to use:

   A = Compliance is high. There are times when you have to give reminders about the expectation, but otherwise it has taken hold as a functioning rule in your home or classroom.

   B = Compliance is tolerable, but not as much as you would like. To get optimal results, you would have to give frequent reminders, plead, or mildly scold the child(ren).

C = Compliance is spotty. You can get results with a lot of effort and heavy-handedness, but generally speaking, this expectation is not working well.

D = Compliance is practically nonexistent. It feels pretty futile to expect any change in behavior in the immediate future.

Next let's look at the demands children make of you.

Every parent or teacher is subject to unacceptable requests from children; permission to engage in some activity or be with some friends, calls for your assistance or attention, food treats, new possessions, suspension of rules, or the use of your property are just a few of the categories to consider. Make a list of unacceptable requests you have received from children.

Unacceptable Requests	Grade
a.	
b.	
c.	
d.	
e.	
f.	
g.	
h.	
i.	
j.	

Grade each request with this system:

A = You have been able to give a firm no to this kind of request. Moreover, your refusal is generally accepted without undue hassle.

B = You have sometimes felt compelled to compromise or give in more than you would like but you have generally been able to refuse this request. The child(ren) have given you a hard time, but have eventually respected your decision.

C = You have given in on this request more often than not. The battle which has ensued over this request is unpleasant, but sometimes there has been a hint of acceptance for your position.

D = You have almost always felt compelled to go along with the request. The protest you have gotten from the child(ren) is not worth your standing firm on the matter.

Interpreting Activity III

It's hard to tell you what the grade average should be for this activity. You will have to decide for yourself whether or not you are satisfied by the results you got.

More important than average grade is the identification of dos and don'ts or unreasonable requests which give you trouble. Look over the results and pinpoint those items which received the lowest grades. They represent the situations which will likely continue to frustrate you in the future unless you take some action. We make this prediction because all of us have a tendency to get caught up in a reactive stance to children's behaviors that disappoint us. Overwhelmed by it all, we sit back in the hope that the child will change, only to find that the next time the behaviors occur we have no new approach to deal with them and are forced once again to operate from the seat of our pants.

To avoid this tendency, we encourage you to take a more assertive stance. Once again go over the items which received low grades and ask this question for each one: *Does it require immediate attention?* As you go through this process, take the attitude that any situation which you do not designate for immediate attention is simply on the back burner for a while. You can come back to it when you are ready. At the same time, assure yourself that those items which you feel require immediate attention are situations in which you really are willing to act to bring about a change. With such a list of priorities, you should then be able to do some active planning rather than always feel like you have to play "catch-up."

We strongly encourage you to keep this limited group of problems in mind as you read the following chapters. Your own situations will help you relate personally to the key ideas and suggestions presented in each chapter. Every chapter may not be specifically relevant to your problems but you will find many concepts and approaches which will improve not only your grades on this activity but your overall effectiveness as a parent or teacher.

4 | Talking Assertively

Communication between adults and children is a back-and forth process. When we tell children what we expect from them or when we react to their behavior, they, in turn, express their acceptance or resistance. If they accept what we have to tell them, the process ends quickly and peaceably. If they resist, the process often feels like a ping-pong game with a seemingly endless volley.

The major reason for resistance is the unpopularity of our request or refusal. "Turn the phonograph down!" may not be what an avid rock fan wants to hear from a parent. Nor is "No, you can't get a drink now" what a thirsty student wants to hear from his teacher. But a number of other elements may be contributing to the resistance as well: our timid voice tone may not conform to the strength of what we are saying; our message may be unclear or accusatory; our words may be repetitive. These components of the message are beyond the content of what we say; communication theorists call them *noise*. This noise, like static on a radio, makes it difficult for children to hear and accept what we're saying.

Many parents and teachers find that their assertiveness is dramatically enhanced if they can reduce noise in their communication with children. For some it has been especially important to alter *what* they actually say to children; for others, it's more the case of *how* they reinforce what they say with their voice, face, and the rest of their body. In this chapter, we will focus on the former. In the next chapter, the emphasis will be on the latter.

There are four basic skills in talking assertively: (1) being direct; (2) being clear; (3) giving reasons freely; and (4) showing interest. Parents and teachers who express directly and clearly what they want from children, who freely convey the reasons for these expectations, and who demonstrate interest in children's points of view are met with far less resistance than adults who lack these skills. Mastery of these skills does not (nor should it) guarantee a conflict-free relationship. Without these skills, however, we appear confused, defensive, arbitrary, and even intimidating to children. That makes the goal of gaining respect for our authority harder to achieve.

All these skills can be learned without special training or instruction. But this learning process may require you to change how you talk to children. Talking differently is like wearing a new pair of shoes. It feels stiff, uncomfortable, and foreign. But if you slowly introduce new ways of talking to children into your style, the process will feel like the leather of those shoes slowly molding themselves to your feet, and you will become comfortable with them.

To help you gain this comfort, we have included exercises after each skill is discussed. They will enable you to practice, to experiment, and to evaluate how you are progressing.

BEING DIRECT

At the heart of talking assertively is the direct expression of feelings and wishes. When we are direct, we are straightforward about what we feel and what we want. We don't beat around the bush; we are to-the-point without being brusque or discourteous. Direct communication conveys an attitude of ownership about one's feelings and wishes. We are in charge of ourselves, we feel free to express what's on our mind, and we are not afraid of conflict. As a result, we don't have to browbeat children to believe we will be heard or send indirect hints of our feelings and wishes to avoid rejection.

The following are examples of direct talk.

- "I'm willing to let you go out tonight if you're home by ten."
- "I need everyone to follow the instructions carefully."
- "The rule is no TV until homework is done."
- "I like it when you tell me where you're going before you leave."
- "I want your work done by three o'clock."
- "I'd like you to pick up the toys you left in the kitchen."
- "I will not check your work until you have a friend check it first."
- "I feel uncomfortable about giving you a make-up lesson."
- "When you leave dirty dishes all over the house, I feel like a maid."
- "I don't like it when you talk before I finish."
- "It's important to me that everyone is listening now."
- "It is time to take a shower."
- "I expect you to wear clean clothes to the party."

There is a wide range of insistence in these statements. Some say emphatically,

- I want
- I will not
- I expect
- The rule is

Others say more provisionally,

- I like it
- I need
- I don't like it
- I feel

What they express in common is that parents or teachers stand behind what they are requesting. There is no attempt to disguise feelings and wishes. Self-acceptance of these feelings and wishes is also present. The speaker refers to himself or herself as the source of these feelings and wishes. The pronoun "I" is frequently used.*

*Note some exceptions like "The rule is" or "It is time . . ." There are situations in which it is preferable to state expectations impersonally. This qualification will be discussed in chapter 7.

For contrast, let's look at some examples of indirect communication.

Imagine a parent, Betty, who asks her daughter, Penny, "Do you want to go to bed now?" hoping to get a positive reply. If Penny says no, Betty then has to counter with, "But Penny, don't you see how tired you are?" in order to get her to bed. Penny is then likely to say something like, "But I'm not tired." Now the discussion will probably have to continue awhile until Penny finally asks, "Do I *have* to go to bed?" Only then might Betty take a direct stand on the matter. Betty's timid question, "Do you want to go to bed now?" has trapped her into a power struggle with Penny. All this might have been avoided if Betty had directly expressed from the start that she wanted Penny in bed.

Asking questions instead of making statements is one way we are indirect. We use this strategy to preserve our "good guy" image with children. Unfortunately, it almost never works, because we get hooked into being an authority figure anyhow ("Do I *have* to go to bed?").

Typically, the questions we ask to avoid direct statements are rhetorical; we don't expect an answer but feel it's kinder to put our thoughts into question form. Let's say a student (David) is rocking back and forth on a chair, trying to show off to his friends that he can do silly things in the classroom. His teacher says in an exasperated voice, "David, can't you sit still?" David smiles to his friends as if to say, "Got him mad, eh?" They giggle with delight as David settles his chair with a slow, clownish motion.

The teacher lost this little game, and he didn't even know he was playing! Had he directly stated something like, "David, that rocking is really annoying. I want you to stop it," the chances are no game would have ensued.

We use all sorts of phrases to introduce rhetorical questions:

- Don't you think you . . . (should clean up now?)
- Why don't you . . . (get your coat on?)
- Would you like to . . . (help with the dishes?)
- How about . . . (going to Grandma's with us?)
- Won't you . . . (baby-sit for us?)

Regardless of the phraseology chosen, the effect is always the same: Our message is not forceful and can be easily manipulated by the child.

Another device we use to avoid taking a direct stand is to focus on the child rather than on what we want from him; instead of stating or restating our expectations, we make adverse comments about the child's present behavior. Although this tactic is used to gain leverage with the child, it often stiffens the child's resistance. For example, to a child who fails to utter "thank you" we might say, "You know, you must be in a world of your own!" Such an indirect statement tries to shame a child into compliance. Usually, it merely ups defensiveness.

The tactic of focusing on the child is also used when we are uncomfortable about owning our feelings of anger. Instead of talking directly about our anger, we often cover it by accusing the child of some flaw in his personality.

Assume it's Sunday and a brother and sister, Joel and Debby, are playing so noisily that they wake up their baby sister in the middle of her daily nap. They know how important it is to be quiet in the vicinity of the baby's room but have lately been quite forgetful about this. Their father, Marty, is livid (especially because it's his turn at child care) and yells out, "You idiots! How many times do you need to be told to keep quiet during the baby's nap? You're both totally self-centered!"

Well, maybe that wasn't a direct expression of Marty's feelings but he surely got his message across. But what message did he convey? Marty actually communicated his "case" against his children. He is claiming proof now that they are clearly in the wrong and thus, justifying his anger. This begs the question: Why does he need to justify his anger? Any father in this situation has a right to be angry. By spending so much energy justifying this right, all Marty succeeds in doing is telling his children they are self-centered idiots. If he wants Debby and Joel to respect his needs (and the baby's), Marty would have been better off saying, "Now that the baby is awake, my afternoon is loused up, and I really resent it. We're going to figure out right now how this can stop, once and for all!"

Because the power adults hold over children can be substantial, there are some important limits to the use of direct talk. For example, we are often asked: "How insistent should my message be when I want children to change their behavior? Should I emphatically say 'I expect you to . . .' or should I limit myself to expressing only feelings about the matter (and avoid indicating how a child should respond to them)?" This concern stems from the advice given by Dr. Thomas Gordon that children will listen to us better if we confront them with our feelings but not our demands (for example, "I don't like cleaning up after you" versus "I expect you to clean up before dinner."). He also believes that children are more likely to assume responsibility for their behavior if given the opportunity to judge how to respond to an adult's concerns.

One suggestion is to consider whether we want to risk leaving the response to our feelings up to a child's discretion. For example, "I worry when you're not home on time" allows a child to figure out how to ease our worry. He might offer to call if he'll be late, or promise to be home promptly next time, or explain that there is no need to worry, etc. However, if we want our worry eased by a plan which virtually guarantees his being on time, we need to specify this clearly. Our needs may otherwise go unheeded and we may leave the child feeling guilty and without direction.

Another question we are asked is whether there are times when it is inappropriate to disclose our feelings about a child's behavior. We believe there are. Direct expression of adult feelings, especially to young children, can be discouraging and rejecting. Being "up front" with children is therefore a risk. Often it is well worth taking; let's look at two examples when it may not be.

Jenny, a nine-year-old, is asked to dress up as a famous person for a school costume party. Her mother offers her an outfit which would be perfect to portray a famous female TV commentator. Jenny's independence and sense of self-reliance is important to her. She rejects the mother's offer and decides to make up her own costume resembling a glamorous actress. After a half an hour of trial and error behind a closed bedroom door, she emerges in her costume, bubbling with pride and excitement and asks, "How do you like it?" The mother is aghast because Jenny looks nothing like the person to be portrayed and is sure Jenny's classmates will laugh at her costume. The mother could share these feelings directly, but there are certainly other viable choices. She might decide, for instance, that it's time for some tactful praise like, "I'm really proud you put it together all by yourself" and a small touch of advice: "Some kids might not know who you are." [Offer one piece of your clothing.] "Would you like my . . . ?"

One of Mr. Stewart's students has little self-confidence. He quits soon after tackling anything but the easiest work. Mr. Stewart feels totally frustrated in his attempts to boost the child's ego and help the child develop the feeling that he can do it. This may not be the time for self-disclosure. The student needs Mr. Stewart's encouragement (although it does not have to be constant). To intrude with feelings of frustration could be detrimental. Mr. Stewart might do well to keep them inside.

As shown in these cases, the most helpful way to talk does not mean disclosing everything on our minds. We need to be selective about where, when, and how feelings are discharged. But it is also important to avoid the other extreme of keeping children in the dark about feelings aroused in us by their actions. Secrecy should not be mistaken for politeness. We sometimes convince ourselves that a child or group of children is too "sensitive" to hear our feelings and wishes. In actuality, we may be afraid of such a child or group—afraid they will get angry at us, retaliate, or make our life difficult. Worst of all, we may fear that we'll lose their approval and love. If we were to test these fantasies with some direct talk, we might find that we don't have so much to fear.

To help you assess your skills of being direct, try these exercises:

1. Translate the following indirect statements to direct ones. Remember to express clearly and honestly your feelings or preferences.

EXAMPLE:

> *(Indirect):* "Why can't you ever come home on time?"
>
> *(Direct):* "I've been very unhappy about your coming home late. I expect you to be on time."

Why don't you tell your sister you're sorry?

Don't you realize that I can't give a make-up test anytime someone's absent?

You're always taking things without asking first.

Some students are awfully restless today.

---

2. Focus on a child with whom you have conflict. Say to yourself the recurring messages you send to that child, i.e., the things you say, over and over again (for example, "Can't you see I'm on the phone?"). Take note of the messages which are expressed indirectly. Imagine that child is in the same room as you are in now. Tell him or her as many feelings, wishes, or complaints that come to your mind as possible. Try to make each expression of a feeling or wish *direct*. Refer back to pages 48 & 49 for help in formulating direct messages.

3. Keep a small pad or set of index cards handy and jot down whenever you get a feeling you want to express to a child (or group of children) but *don't*. Monitor your censoring in this way for two or three days. Then evaluate your list, asking yourself why you held in your feelings each time. You can use the following set of statements as a guide.

- I did not want to discourage (child's name)_____.
- I did not want to hurt (child's name)_____ feelings.
- I was afraid (child's name)_____ would put up a fuss.
- I felt it was easier to handle the matter myself.
- I didn't want to start an argument.
- I was concerned that (child's name)_____ wouldn't understand me.

In which situation do you feel you should have expressed your feelings? Consider whether it is still possible to do so.

BEING CLEAR

Being direct helps the child know *who* is the source of the thoughts and feelings he must reckon with. Being clear reduces noise about *what* is being said.

When we are being clear, we describe in some detail what we want and feel. We don't use vague or abstract words; we are exacting and concrete without being overly talkative. Clear communication conveys an attitude of guidance and helpfulness. We provide the essential information to allow a child to be maximally responsive to us.

We tend to be vague rather than clear when we are unsure what we want from children. Our vagueness leaves children confused or allows them to slough off what we say. A child's physical appearance is a good case in point. In times of constantly changing styles and norms, taking a stand about a child's hair length or taste in clothing is difficult. We may be decidedly unhappy over the choices a child makes but we're not sure if we want to demand conformity to our preferences. Therefore, we might consistently send vague messages like:

- "I don't know what to tell you anymore about your hair."
- "Could you wear something nicer?"
- "I just don't like the way your hair looks."
- "You just don't look right."

Or we might change our message from one day to the next. On Monday, we might complain in great detail about how our child looks, but on Tuesday, we may make it appear that her manner of dress is fine with us.

One of the truly difficult times to know what to say is when a child makes a seemingly reasonable request and we have little more than a gut feeling to refuse it. This happens when the consequences for granting the request are not clear to us, but our intuition tells us to say no. For many adults, this can occur when children ask to sleep over at someone's house, or want to cook something special. In these cases, it is easy to get flustered and mumble "maybe" or "we'll see," leaving the matter up in the air.

While we can't entirely eliminate vagueness, we would do well to lessen it. Two suggestions may be of help. One is to anticipate times we need to take a position about something and try to formulate in our minds what we want to do. Do we want to go along or do nothing? Do we want to provide options? Do we want to insist on a particular course of action? With any of these alternatives, *the important thing is to get clear ahead of time*. The second suggestion is to honestly tell children when we are not sure what we want. This can be done quite assertively: "I'm not sure if I want to give you permission to sleep over at Karen's house. I'll think it over and let you know in fifteen minutes." Or, "The way we get ready for gym just doesn't work. I'll have to think about what we need to do and let you know. If you have any suggestions, please tell me."

Even when we know what we want to say, we can too easily

assume that a few words, certain terms, or a particular glance or frown communicates what is on our mind. This assumption may stem from a belief that if children really cared about us, they would know what we need from them without having to tell them explicitly. Or our assumption may be based on the faulty logic that if we've told children many times what's expected of them, our expectations must be clear to them. On the contrary, we need to be as specific as possible (even if it means physical demonstrations) so children understand what we expect. As a dividend, we should find that specific language has more impact and receives greater respect than does general language. The examples below illustrate the contrast between general and specific talk:

- "I want you to eat foods that are healthy for you like eggs, cheese, fruit, vegetables, and unsweetened drinks," as opposed to, "I wish you would eat better."
- "When we have this discussion, class, it's important to listen to each other and let everyone finish what he has to say," as opposed to, "I want everyone to show good manners in this discussion."
- "Scott, today is your turn to clear the kitchen table. That means putting food back in the refrigerator and dishes in the dishwasher," as opposed to, "Scott, today is your turn to clear the kitchen table. Do it right this time!"
- "Class, I want you to watch the assembly, not talk during it. If you have something you want to share about the program with the person next to you, whisper it [demonstrate with voice] and go back to watching the program," as opposed to, "Class, I want you to cooperate during the assembly."
- "Lately you have a frown on your face or you look away when we talk to you. Is anything the matter?" as opposed to, "Lately you seem unfriendly. What's wrong?"

Another approach to ensure that we are understood is to develop a joint language with children. The more certain words and expressions are shared, the more clear communication tends to become. Words to describe people's actions and feelings are especially worth teaching children. Some words to consider teaching children are:

distracted	responsible	tense	control
left out	defensive	resent	accepting
put down	threatening	plan	trusting
confident	stubborn	begrudge	willing

Some expressions to teach are:

- exploring the alternatives
- taking responsibility for yourself
- putting yourself in somebody else's place
- showing goodwill
- living with things you can't change
- putting someone on the defensive

None of these words or expressions has to be taught in a formal way; it is often best to teach them when they are needed and then repeat them until they become second nature. For example, a participant in one of our recent workshops reported that her nine-year-old son ascribed negative motives to every action she took. Instead of being negative herself about her son's criticalness, she used this opportunity to teach the expression "giving the benefit of the doubt" and found that she and her son both felt better about her teaching what she wanted instead of preaching about it. After this incident, they used the expression whenever it was useful.

Some pet expressions which enable both parties to understand complex communications in a good-natured way can also be taught to children. The examples below have worked for some people. We encourage you to create your own. Compose them together with the children or teach one you make up so that it's understandable to them. Without an appropriate introduction to shorthand communication, these expressions could sound like sarcasm.

- "You left me at McDonalds" *(when either of you could not follow what the other was saying)*
- "We only go around once in life *(when you are not willing to say something more than once)*
- "Those are fighting words" *(when a person has said something that can evoke anger in another person)*

- "Sidney did it again!" *(when you find a mess but you don't know who did it and you want to avoid blaming anyone)*

It is evident that being clear requires more thought than being vague. But because none of us can think quickly on our feet all the time, it makes sense to select important communications in which clear language is critical. And the more you practice being explicitly clear, the easier it gets.

One final thought on clear communication. It can seldom hurt to inquire whether we have been understood. We can do this by asking, "Was I clear?" or, "It's important you know what to do. Do you have any questions?" or, "Could you tell me what I just said so that I know you got it?" Be careful to avoid being insincere or insulting or else children will not respond.

Here are some exercises for developing clear communication:

1. Change the following general statements to make them more specific. Use your own experiences to help you create the details.

EXAMPLE:
> *(General):* Come on, now! Grow up!
> *(Specific):* Hey! I really want you to try to accept what just happened and not cry about it.

I would like you to behave during recess.

_____

I want you and your brother to get along better.

_____

I'd like you to try harder today.

_____

Please clean up the mess in the bathroom.

_____

2. Identify two recent situations in which you believe you have been vague. For each situation, think out a message which is more specific. Write them down below and try them out with your children.

a. _____

_____

b. _____

_____

3. Make a list of requests you anticipate receiving in the next week from your children or students. Take the time now to think out how you want to respond, so your response will be as clear and assertive as possible. The following list might include requests you anticipate, or may help you to identify other ones that may arise:

AT HOME

- an increase in allowance
- a new bed time
- sleeping over at a friend's house
- buying a new record, pair of jogging shoes, etc.
- permission to go somewhere
- use of a parent's possession (e.g. car, stereo)
- eating junk food

AT SCHOOL

- more time to complete an assignment
- to be chosen for some special privilege
- help with completing some task
- less homework
- your opinion on some controversial issue
- specific information about the contents of the next test
- a new seating arrangement, desk, group assignment, etc.

GIVING REASONS FREELY

A big source of grief for parents and teachers is giving reasons for why they want something or why they are refusing a child's request. It makes good sense to give children reasons for our actions. And yet we might find that giving reasons sometimes makes matters worse; it just leads to counterarguments by children. Moreover, no parent or teacher wants to feel obligated to have good reasons for every decision they render. We would be hard pressed to go through a day always attaching reasons to everything we request or deny. But our guess is that the more parents or teachers accompany this talk with reasons, the more likely they will be *respected by* children. Our giving reasons, if done honestly, communicates *respect for* children. We show we care about their right to know why.

This attitude can be communicated even when the child does not understand the reason given. For instance, we might tell a young child, "You can eat that cookie in the kitchen. Living rooms are not for eating." While the child may not grasp the difference in function between the two rooms, simply saying, "You don't eat that cookie here" is less effective. Everything possible should be done to convey to children that our requests are not arbitrary.

Following a request or refusal with a reason also serves to emphasize what we are saying. We appear more assertive simply by putting this extra energy into our communications. Giving a reason suggests to children that we are very certain about our stand and want them to take us seriously. At the same time, by offering more information, we avoid giving children the impression that unquestioned obedience to a tersely stated order is required.

We need to be very careful, however, to give reasons to children nondefensively. Adults who feel they must justify their actions or else lose face are detracting from, rather than enhancing, their assertions. For instance, a teacher might say, "I'd like your work to be neat. I know your teacher last year wasn't a stickler for neatness, but that's the way I am. I'm sorry. OK?" Such apologies don't help gain acceptance, but tend instead to project a pleading, nonassertive stance.

Another mistake is to argue excessively with a child who has not accepted our reason. Trying to convince a child often communicates a lack of respect for his point of view and can also cause even more conflict. For example, take a child who wants to watch a violent TV program against the parent's wishes and the following ensues:

Parent: I don't want you to watch that program. It's too violent.
Child: Oh, come on! The violence doesn't bother me.
Parent: You can't say that. Can't you see that violent shows are bad for all kids?
Child: Not me.

Parent: That's ridiculous. Ever notice how you can't sleep so well after that show?

Child: Where did you get that idea? Come on, I want to see it. It's the best program on TV.

Parent: It may be the most popular program but that doesn't make it the best.

Child: You watch shows like that.

In the parent's attempt to convince the child, she has created a ludicrous trap. Unless the child concedes that she is right, the parent can not feel justified in stopping him from watching the program.

Results are much better if we give reasons with the intent to help children accept adult authority rather than plead for or insist on acceptance. Such reasoning is expressed most effectively when we give reasons freely, as if we want to volunteer information rather than feel compelled to provide it. Note the straightforward, nondefensive spirit of the following comments:

- "Please start your report now. I don't want you to wait until the last minute and do a rushed job."
- "Please finish breakfast. There's not much time to get ready for school."
- "No, I won't let you play because you haven't finished your work."

One way we can help ourselves give reasons freely is to concentrate on helping a child reflect on the needs of a situation. This reflection is facilitated by explaining, in a matter-of-fact way, the consequences of behaviors:

- "When you use up all the milk and don't tell me, I have no way of knowing we need more."
- "By getting into that fight, you blew off a lot of steam, but nothing changed between the two of you."

Another hint for presenting reasons freely is to disclose *personal* reasons for requests that are made for our *personal* benefit. Whenever we disguise our own stake in a situation by moralizing or preaching, we are bound to be more defensive and less helpful. Children will probably be more receptive to honest reasons such as: "Your room needs to be cleaned up. I want it to look nice," or, "I would appreciate it if you were all ready to leave school at exactly 3:30 today. I have a very important faculty meeting and I want to be sure that I get there on time."

Improving the way we give reasons is no guarantee, of course, that what we say will always be accepted. The assertive approach to take when our reasons don't help is simply to stand by our position rather than get into an endless debate. This posture is particularly important when we are confronted with what Rudolf Dreikurs, a noted child psychologist, refers to as *power drunk* children. These are children whose self-esteem depends on convincing themselves that they are worthwhile only if they can boss others around. Heightening their interest in a battle of wills needs to be avoided. Such children have the ability to achieve considerable power by virtue of their capacity to be unreasonable. They use this unreasonableness as a way to bottleneck our attempts to reason with them. In such cases, we would be far better off to avoid going into reasons.

For example, there's a student who keeps wanting to go to the bathroom. His teacher is aware that these bathroom visits are for the purpose of fooling around and getting out of classwork. He asks the teacher for the fourth time in one morning if he can go to the bathroom:

Teacher: No, you've gone three times already. It's obvious you don't need to go.
Student: No, I really got to go!
Teacher: I'm sorry. It's important for you to stay in class and do your work.
Student: I can't help it if I have to go. It's like having to cough. Give me one good reason why I can't go!

At this point, no matter what the teacher says will be counterargued by the student. Knowing this, there could be a strong urge on the part of the teacher to rid himself of this nuisance by an aggressive threat. A simpler and more assertive response would be, "I have already given you my reason."

Here are exercises for working on giving reasons freely:

1. Give a possible reason for each of the requests given below. Try to make the reason as clear and as honest as possible.

EXAMPLE:
> "Please shut the refrigerator door. We use
> more electricity to keep our food cold when
> the door is left open a lot."

a. I'd like you to line up at the door for gym.

_____

b. I want you to work out this argument between you and your
sister by yourselves.

_____

c. Please stop eating with your fingers.

_____

d. There can be no talking during the test.

_____

2. Keeping track of how often you fail to provide a reason for a
request you make or a refusal you give to a child's request can
be a real eye-opener. To monitor yourself, select a time interval
(for instance, every day, three times a week, once a week) for
which you would be willing to look at your reason-giving behavior. You may choose one of the three statements below to describe yourself over the period of time you select.
   a. I almost never remembered to give reasons for my demands
   nor did I explain why I refused requests my children made.
   b. I remembered on occasion, but I have to really think about
   it to do it.
   c. I'm picking up the habit!
3. Parents and teachers sometimes acquiesce to a child's request
or back off their own demands because they fear they do not
have a satisfactory reason. When they do take action, it is often
justified by a lengthy explanation. If you identify with this
problem, it would be helpful for a short period of time to practice making and denying requests without explanation. Select
a time when you feel reasonably calm and confident. Whenever
you wish to make or deny a request, try to do so clearly and
firmly. If a brief reason for your actions comes to mind, share
it with the child(ren) if you *want to*. But whenever you feel that
you *have to* give a reason, be very careful to state your request

or response without explanation. Assess how you feel during this time and how your children respond to you. Are you more aware of the difference between volunteering reasons and feeling compelled to give reasons?

SHOWING INTEREST

Many people believe that adults cannot be firm and friendly with children at the same time. Some children, they contend, take advantage of adult friendship and use it to get away with as much mischief as possible; some even find ways to use their own love and approval as a weapon whenever they do not get their way.

There are communication skills we can utilize to both assert authority and maintain a close, friendly relationship with children. These skills help us show interest in what children think and feel. *Showing interest* is the companion of *giving reasons.* Giving reasons is sharing our side of a conflict; showing interest is responding to the child's side.

There are three major subskills of showing interest. They are *checking out, empathizing,* and *acknowledging.* We will discuss them one at a time and then look at how they can be used in the same situation to enhance our relationship with children.

Checking Out

When children object to something we've said or done, it is often helpful to check out our understanding of their feelings. Checking out can be done in a wide range of ways, from simply asking for clarification to playing a hunch about what a child is feeling. Below are examples:

Child: I don't want to go to her party.
Parent: Why don't you want to go?

Student: Do we have to diagram sentences again?
Teacher: I'm not sure if you feel that it's hard or boring or just silly. What do you feel?

Child: You're mean!
Parent: My guess is you can't believe I said no. Am I right?

Student: I can't do this stuff.
Teacher: Do you want to call it quits for just now or do you really feel hopeless about it?

Checking out serves several useful purposes:

- It lets children know we want to receive what they have to say.
- It avoids misunderstanding.
- It allows for reflection during a heated battle.
- It communicates to children that we are not threatened by their feelings (even if they are negative and harsh).
- It permits us to explore children's motives without being mindreaders.
- It helps children clarify their feelings.

It's important that our desire to check out is genuine. Otherwise we can quickly lose a child's trust. A check-out question should not be rhetorical. "What's wrong with diagramming sentences?" is really an *indirect* way of saying, "I don't agree with your feelings." A check-out question should not be used unless we are prepared to accept the answer. Notice how this teacher is unaccepting.

Student: I can't do this stuff.
Teacher: Do you want to call it quits for just now or do you really feel hopeless about it?
Student: I'll never get it. I've had it for this stuff.
Teacher: Aren't you ever going to try something hard?

Even if our intention is sincere, children can still be suspicious. So we have to be careful how we express our check-out question. When we ask, "Why don't you want to go to the party?" we can invite the child's trust by adding, "I'd really like to understand your feelings about the party."

Empathizing

Empathy is the expression of appreciation or recognition for feelings of another person. Empathizing with children's viewpoints is an important responsibility. It helps children know that their feelings are real and that we respect them.

Empathizing should not be confused with agreeing. *From our point of view,* we may not agree at all with a child's viewpoint. We might not feel or experience things the same way if we were in their shoes. Nonetheless, it is possible and helpful to convey that we recognize their position and that it may make sense *from their point of view.*

Showing empathy can have a definite benefit for adults. When we empathize with children, they can be amazingly receptive to our authority. The power of empathy should, therefore, not be misused.

In the following examples, notice how empathy is expressed:

A child is watching a baseball game on TV. His father approaches the child to inform him that it is dinnertime.

Father: It's time to come in for dinner.

Child: Can't I watch a little longer? It's the eighth inning and the score is tied.

Father: I know it's hard to leave an exciting game. I'd probably want to stay and watch it if I liked baseball as much as you, but this *is* the time for dinner. The food is ready.

A student is arguing with a teacher about a wrong answer on a multiple choice test. She is convinced her answer is also correct.

Student: I don't see how I got number six wrong. I'm sure they speak Spanish in Brazil.

Teacher: I can see why you think so. In most countries in South America, people speak Spanish. But in Brazil, they speak Portuguese.

Student: But I'm *sure* I'm right!

Teacher: Well, I can believe that. Sometimes it doesn't seem possible to be wrong when something makes sense. Will you take my word for it or should we check in a reference book?

Acknowledging

In their conflicts with us, children often take us by surprise by making very effective criticisms of our actions. There is no reason why we have to feel embarrassed by this circumstance. Rather than a wordy apology or confession of shortsightedness, we can simply acknowledge the validity of their point of view and, if we believe it's warranted, change our stand. Many times, however, children's valid points are just that—valid points. They believe that one good point wins an argument. It is difficult for them to understand that our judgments result from mature, experienced thinking, even when our logic is not perfect or our explanations ironclad.

In such situations, we can avoid needless arguments by acknowledging children's thinking before proceeding to explain our perspective. The extent to which we do this can be as minor as acknowledging a small kernel of truth in their position, or as major as a whole-hearted agreement. Here are some examples:

Parent: I don't want you riding a skateboard.

Child: Ah, Dad. All my friends ride skateboards and none of them has gotten hurt.

Parent: That is true. I simply don't want to take a chance. Accidents *do* happen on skateboards.

Child: Of course, and from driving cars, too.

Parent: Yes, that's also true. It's just that there's less chance with a car.

Teacher. Sally, you do your worksheets much too quickly.

Student: But I get most everything right.

Teacher: Well, I guess I would agree with that. I'm concerned that it's a bad habit to get into. You can make mistakes that way.

Student: Lots of kids do their worksheets quickly.

Teacher: *(Pauses and then replies)* You know, you're right. I think it would be a good idea if we talked about this at the next class meeting. Maybe we could work out some understanding that we'd all be happy with.

All three skills—checking out, empathizing, and acknowledging—can be effectively interwoven. We will illustrate with a family situation and a classroom episode.

1. There has been considerable friction in the Taylor family over the use of the telephone. Mr. Taylor is especially upset that his

teenage son and daughter, Jon and Gail, talk on the phone so much that few other calls can get through. They are talking about the problem at dinner.

Father: I am still upset over this phone problem. Last night one of my friends tried for two hours to reach me. Do you agree that I have a legitimate gripe? (checking out)

Gail: Ah, come on. It's not as bad a problem as you say it is.

Father: Well, it doesn't happen every night (acknowledging), but when it does happen, we all get angry at each other.

Jon: Can't we get one of those phones which lets you know when someone is calling you while you're talking to someone else?

Father: I can understand how that would solve the problem for you and Gail (empathizing), but I am concerned that it would be costly. Do you think it's the only solution we've got? (checking out)

Gail: Well, we could just try very hard to talk on the phone less, but I don't think it will really work.

Father: You're being pretty honest (acknowledging). Let's just see what happens. Maybe we'll need special phone times for you and Jon if you can't cut down by yourself. Let's see how you do. OK?

Both: OK, Dad.

2. A sixth-grade teacher is upset that behind her back, three boys in her classroom have been using offensive language. She asks to meet with them about it.

Teacher: I am hoping we can work out a problem that has been bothering me. You have been using words like "shit" or "fuck" when you think I can't hear it. I'm uncomfortable with language like that in this classroom.

Student: We don't do it that much.

Teacher: Are you saying that it should not be a problem for me or that you haven't talked that way so much? (checking out)

Student: I don't see anything wrong with it.
Teacher: Well, you have a perfect right to feel that way (empa-
           thizing). Different people have different opinions
           about these words. I just don't want them in this
           classroom. It can get out of hand and I don't want
           that to happen.
Student: Adults talk that way a lot.
Teacher: You're right, they do (acknowledging). I just don't
           want it here. Fair enough?
Students: OK.

To help you develop skills in checking out, empathizing, and
acknowledging, these exercises are suggested:
1. For each of the following statements, compose a check-out question which helps to clarify what the child has said.

EXAMPLE:
           "I can't fall asleep. Can I stay up and watch
           TV?"
           (Response): "Is there another way to help
           you fall asleep?"

Danny keeps calling me names.

_____

Do I have to clean this up all by myself?

_____

I don't see why we have to go over something we already learned.

_____

I don't want to go to art.

_____

2. For each of the following statements, compose a statement
   which empathizes with the feelings of the child.

EXAMPLE:
           "I don't want to play with her. She always
           plays with dolls."

(Response): "That must not be too much fun
for you."

I don't have time to change my clothes. Chris is waiting
for me.

_____

All the other teachers let us talk during a test.

_____

I want to sit in the front seat when we go on our family trip today.
Jane always gets to sit up front.

_____

I'm old enough to make my own decisions about what clothes I
wear!

_____

3. The adversary relationship between adults and children
prompts many battles between the two sides. It is difficult to
refrain from countering every argument a child makes with one
of our own. The following responses are helpful when a child
has made a valid point in a verbal conflict between you. Experiment with them to find the ways in which it is most comfortable
for you to acknowledge the validity of what a child says. Make
up your own ways to express acknowledgment.

- "I see what you mean."
- "That's true."
- "You've got a good point."
- "You're right."
- "That makes sense."
- "That could be."
- "I think I would see it that way also if I were you."

SUMMING UP

The four basic skills we have presented here—being direct,
being clear, giving reasons freely, and showing interest—form the
foundation of assertive adult authority. Too often, parents and
teachers abandon their efforts to improve in these areas when the

payoff is not immediate. Don't make this mistake. Give yourself a chance to gain effectiveness in talking assertively. Practice the skills and then examine how each works best for you. If you find, however, that talking assertively is not eventually getting the results you want, the advice given in the next two chapters may be especially helpful.

5 | Behaving Assertively

"I say all the right words but either the children are deaf or I'm not being taken seriously."

"I thought my daughter and I were having a rational discussion about curfews. I wasn't trying to scold or shame her but she got very defensive and angry. She took everything I said the wrong way."

"I said exactly the same thing as Mrs. Smith. She got the attention of the class but I didn't. I guess some people just have what it takes."

At one time or another, all of us have felt misunderstood or ignored when we talk with children. Our words seem clear and direct but somehow the message gets distorted. Because so many of us have experienced this difficulty, a belief has grown up about why these miscommunications occur.

Many of us believe that good parents and teachers are naturals. These adults are said to have certain innate skills and abilities that cannot be taught to others. Some teachers just *know* how to keep order in a classroom and how to keep children interested in learning. Some parents just *know* how to relate to their children, and how to discipline them effectively. In our experience working with parents and teachers, we do meet people who seem to be naturals. However, when we watch them closely, we observe that their success is related, in large measure, to their skill in using nonverbal behaviors to enhance their relationships with children. There is no mystery that accounts for their success. The naturals have learned these nonverbal behaviors and we can learn them too. The following examples may help to demystify this process.

It's 8:30 on a Friday morning. The ninth-grade class has just begun to recite the Pledge of Allegiance. Many students are giggling, talking, and clowning around. The room is noisy and charged with frivolous excitement. Teacher A is annoyed with the class. Her goal is to quiet them, complete this morning exercise and begin the day's lesson. She frowns, puts her hands on her hips, and stares straight ahead. She interrupts the recitation and shouts over the din, "I know it's hard to be *serious* on Friday mornings, class. Let's begin *again.*" In order to be heard, her voice is loud and her tone is sarcastic. Those in her limited line of vision quiet down but the others continue fooling around and poking one another.

Teacher B, in the same situation, stops reciting the Pledge of Allegiance and stands calmly looking around the room. Her eyes scan the class. She is not glaring, but rather looking from student to student. She waits until the room becomes silent and then says, "I know it's hard to be serious on Friday morning, class. Let's begin again." Her voice is relaxed, sympathetic and firm. The class recites the Pledge of Allegiance in an orderly fashion.

A busy mother is talking to a close friend on the telephone. Her six-year-old son runs into the room, grabs his mother's arm and says, "The TV is messed up, Mommy. The picture's all funny. Come and fix it. I'm missing the best part!"

Mother A jerks her son's hand from her arm. Her eyebrows rise as she shakes her head in dismay saying, *"I'm* on the *phone* now. I'll fix it in five minutes. You can wait *five minutes.* Can't you?"

Mother B holds her son's hand gently. She looks at him directly and says, "I'm on the phone now. I'll fix it in five minutes. You can wait five minutes, can't you?" Her voice is soothing. Her face is attentive.

The lesson of these examples is self-explanatory. Teacher and Parent B are more likely to have successful interactions because of what they do while speaking to a class or to a child. Our words are delivered through the medium of nonverbal communication and it's this delivery system which is the crucial factor determining how our words are received and understood.

The expression, "It's not what you say but how you say it that counts," is true. In fact, Albert Mehrabian, one of the most well known researchers in interpersonal communication, concludes that *what* we say accounts for only seven percent of the impact of our message on the person with whom we are talking. Ninety-three percent of how people respond to our message is accounted for by *how* we are behaving nonverbally.*

Through his research, Mehrabian has developed a formula that graphically depicts the importance of nonverbal behavior in the communication process. The formula is:

Total Impact = 7% verbal + 38% vocal + 55% facial

This means that whether a child accepts, respects, or ignores our message is due to what we say (7%), our tone of voice and volume (38%), and the expression on our face (55%).

While they operate much like reflexes, nonverbal behaviors are extremely important in determining whether we are perceived as nonassertive, aggressive, or assertive. But because we are less aware of how we behave nonverbally, we are less able to bring these behaviors under conscious control. Unless we have had the opportunity to see ourselves on videotape, we are probably unaware of the effect of our nonverbal behavior. We can't see and hear ourselves as others can. And yet what others see and hear greatly influences how they respond to us.

In order to become more aware of our nonverbal behaviors, it is helpful to know specifically what to look for. In the following sections, the major nonverbal components of behavior will be described: vocal, facial, postural, and silent communication. Ways to present ourselves more assertively to children are also suggested.

*Albert Mehrabian, *Nonverbal Communication*. (Chicago: Aldine-Atherton, 1972).

VOCAL COMMUNICATION

The vocal components of nonverbal behavior include volume, fluency, inflection, and emotional tone.

Volume

Volume refers to how loudly or softly our message is delivered. SPEAKING LOUDER THAN NECESSARY MAY MAKE CHILDREN FEEL FRIGHTENED. Yelling hurts our ears and is a form of punishment in itself. On the other hand, *speaking too softly may be annoying to a child who must strain to hear us.* If we speak this way, children may not bother to listen to us or may dismiss what we're saying as unimportant.

Fluency

Some! Adults! Speak! In! A! Jack! Hammer! Fashion! The words come fast and each word seems to be punctuated. The child may feel that each word is accompanied by a finger poking at her shoulder. This speech pattern does not flow well and is often perceived as aggressive.

Frequent . . . uh . . . pauses and . . . uneven and . . . uhm . . . halting speech is associated with . . . uh . . . nonassertion. This pattern . . . especially with . . . uh, children . . . whose . . . attention spans are, uhm, short . . . can be annoying and . . . will not be listened . . . to . . . with full attention.

When adults speak in a reasonably fluent fashion, it is easier to listen to them. This does not mean that we have to become an orator in order to communicate effectively with children. However, attention to speed and fluency does help to define our communication as assertive.

Inflection

This next component is important. When people speak, they tend to emphasize some words more than others. Where emphasis is placed changes the meaning and emotional tone of our message. The following example may help to clarify this point.

- *"I* want you to go to bed (!)"
- "I want you to go to *bed (?)*"
- "I want you to go to bed."

The first statement emphasizes the word *I.* By so doing, the meaning of the statement changes from a declaration to an exclamation. Such a statement could be threatening to a child because it tends to emphasize the power distinction in the relationship.

In the second example, the accent is placed on the *bed.* In order to do this, the pitch of one's voice must go up. The sentence becomes a question and may be perceived as nonassertive because it connotes ambivalence, pleading, or doubt.

The final statement is just that—a simple declaration of fact which is firm, clear, and assertive.

Emotional Tone

Children attend more to our tone of voice than to our words. This is understandable because our tone of voice conveys our true feelings more accurately than our words. Sometimes our messages become confusing to children because there is a discrepancy between our words and our emotional tone. Words of anger, for example, are usually associated with a loud voice. When we say to a child, "I'm really annoyed" in a calm voice, the child is understandably confused. Saying "I love you" in the same offhanded way that you would say "Take out the trash" may be perceived as neither real nor caring by the child. The discrepancy between what we say and our emotional tone creates distrust in children. Praise will be seen as empty praise, words of encouragement will be seen as phony, and anger will be discounted.

FACIAL COMMUNICATION

The two major nonverbal components of facial communication are eye contact and facial expression. Eye contact is one of the most basic ways of nonverbally communicating interest, respect, firmness, confusion, anger, and a host of other emotions. Our eyes are extremely important clues to understanding the meaning of our words.

Think about the facial expressions that accompany the following feelings. Use a mirror to watch the way your expression changes and think about how other people might perceive the expressions.

- Attentive and concerned
- Firm but approachable
- Uninterested
- Disgusted
- Confused and uncertain
- Angry and threatening
- Loving and proud

As you will probably discover from this exercise, our eyes and facial expression are connected. It's difficult to glare at someone without tensing the rest of our face and it's hard to look firm yet approachable without a relaxed facial expression. The emotion expressed by our eyes and face is, according to Mehrabian, the primary factor in determining people's responses to our communication. Children are very aware of facial expressions. Whether children will continue to pester us with unreasonable demands, whether they will do what we ask, or whether they will feel loved and respected is as dependent on how we look at them as on what we say.

POSTURAL COMMUNICATION

Our hand gestures, body stance, physical position in relation to a child, and the physical distance between us and that child also contribute to the child's response.

Hand Gestures

Hands can point, pound, fidget, and make fists. They can say "come closer" or "go away." They can express praise, disgust, or confusion. For example, a father who finds that his daughter has broken a glass vase could throw up his hands in disgust, shake his fist in anger, make fists with both hands and put them on his hips, put his hands to his head, wring his hands in dismay, or gesture with open hands as if inquiring about what happened. Without saying a word, this father can clearly convey to his daughter his reaction to the situation.

Body Stance

Carrying this scene a bit farther, the father's body posture will give clues to his reaction as well. In one response, he might cross his arms in front of his chest, tense his neck muscles, lock his knees, and glare. In another response, he could begin to pace, flail his hands aimlessly in the air, shift from one foot to the other, and lower and shake his head. These two descriptions send very different messages to a child. The first conveys anger, the second, confusion and dismay. A third alternative might be to stand with his feet slightly apart, hands by his side, looking directly at the child. This body stance would be most likely to convey firm, nonaccusatory assertion.

We often add to the natural problems of communication by responding in ways that may instigate further misbehavior by the child. In the first example, the father's body language might heighten defensiveness and argumentative behavior in his daughter. Father Two may get an "I'm sorry, Dad. I'll try to be more careful" response in order to placate him. But the likelihood of the child's repeated transgression is increased, because Dad was not really firm but, in fact, seemed helpless to deal with the situation. An assertive posture heightens the possibility of discussion and a mutually agreed upon resolution of the situation.

Distance

Whether we stand close, too close, or far from children also sends messages to them. People in different cultures have rules about the appropriate distance between communicating individuals. Adults in our society generally stand about eighteen to twenty-four inches apart when they converse. This distance varies, however, with the age and type of relationship we have with each other. For example, friends stand closer together than acquaintances and adults tend to stand closer to children than to other adults.

Standing too close to a child may make a child very uncomfortable. This is especially true during a confrontation when standing nose-to-nose with the child adds an unnecessary degree of hostility. Towering over a seated child is similarly threatening.

On the other hand, when we stand in the kitchen and call on a child in the living room to do something, we decrease the likelihood of getting a satisfactory response. When confrontation or disagreement is likely, it is helpful to stand near the child and state our request or concern. When comfort is called for, moving closer to the child is a good idea, as long as we're sensitive to the desires of the child. Kneeling or sitting with a child can reduce the threat of our size.

Touching

Have you ever seen a parent yanking a screaming youngster through a store or a teacher pulling a reluctant student toward the principal's office? Most of us cringe at such a sight. We cringe, but can you imagine the depth of the child's emotional response —fear, helplessness, rage, and embarrassment?

Many people who contend that they never hit a child may be pokers, ticklers, pinchers, or jabbers. All of these forms of touching can convey anger or frustration and heighten the likelihood that similar responses will occur in children. Also, children will resent their parents' indirectness, coyness, or deception.

Although affectionate touching is a very important part of any relationship, it is especially important with children. Infants who are not touched or held affectionately are more likely to become ill and even die than those who are. Touching is not just necessary for infants, however. Human beings of every age need warm physical contact with others. How we express physical affection should vary with the age of the child, but the need for affectionate physical contact does not diminish with age.

While touching can express a multitude of feelings toward a child, there are three ways to touch that enhance our relationships and, consequently, our assertive authority role with children.

- Touching—in the form of anything from a warm pat to an enthusiastic embrace—can be used to express caring, love, empathy, and support.
- Touching—in the form of gently grasping a child's shoulders or holding onto one hand—can help a child listen to us and help us to directly communicate our wishes, requests, and feelings about a child's behavior.
- Touching—in the form of holding a child from behind or hugging—can also be used to calm and gently restrain a child who is very upset or out of control.

SILENCE

Silence is not just the absence of sounds or words. It is a very powerful nonverbal behavior which can express a variety of emotions including anger, concern, support, hurt, pouting, or lack of interest.

Many of us remember coming home late from a date only to be met with stony silence from our parents. Perhaps we got the silent treatment from a teacher when we misbehaved in school. We have no doubt that you can remember scenes similar to these and that you know now, and knew as a child, that the adult involved was angry with you.

On the other hand, silence may be used to express caring, concern, and support. If you remember angry silences, we assume that you also recall supportive silences. A beautiful memory for one of us, involved the use of silence. While visiting a favorite and very loving aunt, my younger sister and I got into an argument. My aunt became angry and scolded me for quarreling. I was hurt that she had reprimanded me and felt guilty for misbehaving. I ran out of the house and sat under the pear tree. For some time I cried, feeling dejected. After a while, Aunt Annie came outside and sat down next to me without saying a word. She just sat looking at the tree and the flowers. I could feel her warmth and caring even though no words were spoken. After about ten minutes, she took a stick of gum from her pocket, broke it, and gave half to me, keeping half for herself. We sat together, chewing, for a few more minutes, and then went in to supper.

This example represents one of many possible ways silence may be used to express support and love for children. Sitting quietly next to a child who is sad or depressed, not intruding with words into children's grief, anger, hurt, or disappointment are means of invoking the healing properties of silence.

When children behave improperly, some of us use silence to pout or express our hurt. The teacher or parent who pouts is adding guilt to other feelings a child may have about his or her behavior. There are some problems with the silent expression of hurt. First, the message that a child receives is that breaking a milk bottle, talking in class, or staying out late are not only against the rules but hurt the parent or teacher. This is a difficult burden to carry. Second, looking hurt or pouting is an indirect expression of feeling. The adult need not have to worry about being an autocrat and directly confronting the offender. Instead, the adult punishes the child by appearing to be the victim of the child's villainy.

Finally, silence can express indifference. When an enthusiastic child runs in the front door to show us a good report card and we don't respond, the child gets an "I don't care" message. When a student raises his hand and the teacher ignores him, the same message of indifference is conveyed.

HOW CAN WE SEE OURSELVES AS OTHERS SEE US?

Although the various kinds of nonverbal behavior have been described separately, they occur together. Our voice, facial expression, posture, position, and hands all respond in concert, gradually developing into patterns and automatic reactions. Performers who do impersonations of famous people capitalize on the nonverbal patterns of the people they imitate. And people who know us are probably more aware of our nonverbal patterns than we are because we can't see our responses as well as others can.

The best way to get information about how we look to others is to ask them. This feedback is most helpful when it is descriptive and specific. There are several ways to get this feedback.

1. Ask a friend, spouse, or another teacher to watch you interacting with children. After fifteen or twenty minutes, sit down with your observer and ask:
a. "What did I look like?"
b. "Were there any nonverbal behaviors of mine that might discourage or alienate a child?"
c. "What did my face (voice tone, posture, hands) convey to you? Could you tell how I was feeling?"
d. "Were there any nonverbal behaviors of mine that made me look like a pushover? Did I seem timid at any time?"
e. "Which of my nonverbal behaviors was most noticeable to you?"
f. "Did my body language match what I was saying? How? If not, what was discrepant?"

2. With two other adults or older children, role play the following situations. One person will role play the child. The other observes you.

a. A student in your classroom is talking and not paying attention. You walk up to her and tell her to pay attention.

b. Your daughter comes home late from school. You tell her that she must come home on time.

c. Your three-year-old refuses to pick up his toys. You want him to do this now because you are having company in half an hour.

d. A student in your class pushes another student on the playground. They begin to fight. You walk up to them and say _____ _____.

e. Your teen-ager has skipped school. The teacher called to tell you this. The teen-ager comes home and you _____ _____.

After each role play, have the observer replay the scene by portraying you as precisely as possible. The observer should do and say exactly what you did and said. The person playing the child can give you feedback on how nonverbal behavior affected him or her.

3. Think of a person whom you would describe as aggressive. There are probably many behaviors of that person that make you think of him or her as aggressive. Make a list of that person's actions. Be as descriptive as possible.

Now think of a person that you would describe as nonassertive or passive. Make a list of that person's actions. Be as descriptive as possible.

Finally, think of another person whom you would describe as assertive. Make a list of that person's actions. Again, be as descriptive as possible. Review all three lists and circle those behaviors that describe you. In which situations would you behave in these ways? How do you feel when you're behaving that way?

4. If possible, tape record a classroom session or discussion with a child. How do you sound? What would you feel like if you were the child or children involved? What do you like or dislike about what you hear?

ASSERTIVE NONVERBAL COMMUNICATION
AND OUR AUTHORITY ROLE

Even when our words are assertive, we often undermine our authority by behaving in nonassertive or aggressive ways. Children, understandably, become confused when our nonverbal and verbal messages are inconsistent. We, on the other hand, become frustrated when children don't appear to take us seriously, ignore us, or misunderstand our intentions.

Behaving assertively helps children know that we mean what we say. They are less likely to persist with unreasonable demands, attempts to get us to change our mind, or other unacceptable behavior if we are clear both verbally *and* nonverbally. Lengthy discussions (or arguments) will be shortened considerably when our words match our actions.

Cutting down the amount of talk time that transpires between adults and children has very positive effects. Adults often feel compelled to explain and re-explain their actions to children. This excessive discussion is time consuming and can trap us into changing our minds, becoming confused, or getting so angry that we overreact and become too punitive. When we talk too much we are likely to increase children's resistance or increase tension and emotional outbursts in them or in ourselves. Learning to be nonverbally assertive helps us to rely less on our verbal abilities and prevents miscommunication and heightened resistance in interactions with children.

DEVELOPING ASSERTIVE NONVERBAL
BEHAVIORS

Even though it is difficult to become aware of your behaviors, and to change such ingrained patterns, it can be done with just a little effort. Actually, you've already begun if you've tried out some of the ideas suggested earlier in this chapter. These activities were designed to help you become aware of your nonverbal patterns. Our guess is that by simply reading this chapter and participating in these activities, some of your behaviors have already changed.

Of course, there will continue to be other behaviors that you might like to change. We've outlined some further steps that you can take to gain more control over your nonverbal behaviors and to develop assertive skills in this important area. A word of caution before we begin: You can't change everything at once. Trying to learn the oboe, flute, drums, and piano all at once would be, to say the least, very tricky. The same is true of behavior. Choose one or two to work on at a time. Once these change to your satisfaction, you can work on others. We've developed a three-step process to help you initiate behavior change.

STEP 1

The charts below outline nonassertive, aggressive, and assertive nonverbal behaviors. Look at each chart and place a star next to the assertive behaviors that you do well. Circle the nonassertive and aggressive behavior that you engage in.

Vocal Nonverbal Behavior

Nonassertive	Aggressive	Assertive
voice too soft	voice louder than necessary	moderate loudness
frequent pauses	fast speech	even speed
filler words (uh, ah)	jack hammer	fluent
questions	exclamatory sentences	declarative sentences

Facial Nonverbal Behavior

Nonassertive	Aggressive	Assertive
little eye contact	glaring, staring	open, direct eye contact
tense facial muscles (fear)	tense facial muscles (anger)	relaxed facial muscles
pleading, timid look	impassive, stony look	confident, engaged look

Postural Nonverbal Behavior

Nonassertive	Aggressive	Assertive
fidgeting, ringing hands	clenched fists	open hands
hands behind back or in pockets	finger pointing	hands at sides
nervous, shifting body	rigid body position	relaxed body position
standing at a considerable distance	standing very close	standing at a respectful distance

Touching Nonverbal Behavior

Nonassertive	Aggressive	Assertive
not touching	grabbing to induce compliance	holding to calm or restrain
nervous touching	poking to make points	touching to aid communication
feeling too timid to comfort or encourage through touch	withholding the comfort or encouragement of touch	touching to comfort or encourage

Silent Behavior

Nonassertive	Aggressive	Assertive
confusing silence	silence treatment	calming silence
pouting	disapproving silence	silence accompanied by action
silent fear	silent disinterest	silent encouragement

STEP 2

Most likely you have starred and circled several behaviors. Because you can't work on all of the circled behaviors at once, choose two behaviors that you feel happen frequently and interfere significantly with your ability to be assertive with children. The two behaviors are:

1._____

2._____

STEP 3

The next step in altering these behaviors is to develop a plan to change them in the direction that you think is necessary to help you become more assertive. Each reader's chosen behaviors will be different, so described below is a sample plan that may aid all readers in developing their own individualized change strategy.

Let's say that you've decided that your lack of eye contact detracts from your ability to be assertive. Your goal, then, is to increase the amount of eye contact you have with your children, and increase your comfort level when you look directly at children.

The first step in achieving this is to remember to work on your goal. Often, the hardest thing to do is to consistently remember to practice a new behavior. For example, when we make the decision to diet it is very easy to forget to do it; we remember that we're dieting after dessert instead of before. This forgetfulness happens because behavior change takes time and energy, while our habitual ways of behavior are easy and comfortable. Consequently, it helps to provide reminders in the form of mental or even written notes.

Now it's important to develop action strategies that will help you increase your eye contact. Some strategies are:
1. Stand or sit directly in front of the child.
2. After a discussion or confrontation with a child, go to another room and try to recall how the child's face looked during your interaction. What was he or she wearing?
3. During an interaction with a child, if you begin to feel that you're losing ground or backing down, check to see if you are maintaining good eye contact.

One final step is often necessary to change behavior and that is thinking assertively. We frequently stop ourselves from achieving our goals by saying things to ourselves which defeat us. For example, we might say things like:

- "If I look at her, I'll melt."
- "I can get my argument together if I look away."
- "I wish I didn't have to face him."

Such thoughts make it very difficult to maintain direct eye contact. Making positive self-statements increases our chances of being successful.

More positive statements might be:

- "Facing them keeps me from running away."
- "Looking helps us see eye-to-eye."
- "Looking helps them hear me."

Our suggestion is to be persistent. Don't be discouraged if you occasionally revert to old patterns. Remember, changes take time and effort.

6 | Avoiding Power Struggles

In the previous two chapters we have suggested to say what you want and how to sound and look like you mean it. But even if you are well on your way toward establishing yourself as an assertive authority figure, you should expect that children will continue to hassle you. A preschooler could insist on wearing the same clothes day in and day out. Second graders may ignore a firm order to cease their endless chatter. A preteen-ager may continue to ask if she can stay up late to watch TV even though she falls apart the next day from inadequate sleep. And high school students may expect extensions on their papers despite the clear reasons given to meet the teacher's deadline.

There is no way that day-to-day conflicts will totally disappear. The problem is how to avoid the loss of all our energy to wasteful power struggles. When energy is in short supply we get cranky and nasty with children or just give up and let them have their way.

Needless power struggles develop when we overreact to children's misbehavior. Some adults, for example, allow themselves to be so upset by defiance or irresponsibility that they loudly draw a battle line every time a child scoffs at their feelings or tries to get them to change their mind. They never back off for a few seconds, or inwardly chuckle at the child's stubbornness, or quietly stand their ground. Instead, they immediately try to convince the child how inappropriate or unreasonable his behavior is or try to bully him into submission. These responses are usually self-defeating and always energy-draining. There is nothing that increases strong-willed children's adrenalin more than when adults entice them into battle.

It is wasteful to fret that children, even very difficult ones, are getting the better of us. What happens is that we grant children more power than they really have. Have you ever said: "My kids are driving me crazy," or "I'll bet other adults don't have to put up with this," or "Why do I deserve this?" When we talk like this, we only hassle ourselves (as well as hassle a spouse, friend, or colleague to whom we tell these thoughts). We can use our available energy to plan how to reduce conflict to a manageable level rather than feel sorry for ourselves.

The key skill in avoiding power struggles is knowing how to remain in a position of self-control when children are resistant. Rather than let children's antics determine our response, we need to be in charge of our own actions. The trick is to be aware of several options for preventing and coping with conflict before it arises so we can choose how to act when it does ensue.

In this chapter we will share with you alternative approaches for avoiding power struggles which at the same time encourage children to change their behavior. Learning and using them should enable you to preserve energy for the other important tasks you face as parents or teachers and even provide some left over energy all for yourself. We don't expect all the approaches cited here to be your cup of tea. But we do predict that your repertoire of coping strategies will be increased.

MAKING RULES EFFECTIVE

The *take charge* way to deal with conflict (and the power struggles which attend it) is to try to prevent its occurrence. Our success at conflict prevention is largely dependent upon the quality of rules we establish for children. Rules are long-term decisions governing such things as a child's

- movement (example rule: No running in the house or classroom.)

- belongings (example rule: Personal possessions can be brought into school on Friday.)
- responsibilities (example rule: The trash must be put out on the street on collection day.)
- relationships (example rule: Disputes between siblings or classmates must be resolved without hitting.)
- living habits (example rule: No candy or cookies can be eaten during the morning.)

Good rules provide children with a secure world. By knowing that there are consistent curbs on their behavior and demands on their shoulders, children gain support in their efforts with self-regulation and impulse control. Adults often feel guilty about being rule makers; they feel less in control when they give on-the-spot directives or spontaneously set limits. The reluctance to establish some long-term rules, however, means that children are denied valuable baselines for their behavior. Rules benefit adults as well, because they allow parents and teachers to assume an active rather than reactive stance in relationship to children's behavior. If we know in advance what our expectations are, they are easier to uphold.

Wise rule making is not a mysterious art.* It involves a few, simple steps:

1. *Make sure that the rule can be made clear both to you and to the child(ren).* As we have previously discussed, it cannot be assumed that a set of words make a rule self-evident. Imagine that we have set a rule that a child must be ready for school before breakfast. What do we mean by *ready?* How does the child know? Does it include having permission slips signed? Receiving lunch money? Hair combed? School books packed and placed by the front door? Rules are not clear when some of these details have not been worked out. Unclear rules lead to conflict; the child believes that he has met the rule but the adult is not satisfied.

2. *Assess whether the rule is enforceable.* It would be foolish to inform children of a rule which we anticipate can't be enforced. If we establish the rule anyhow, there will surely be a constant battle over it. In determining whether or not a rule is enforceable,

*For a good discussion on making rules, see Judith M. Smith and Donald E. Smith, *Child Management: A Program for Parents and Teachers,* (Champaign, Ill.: Research Press, 1976).

there are three test questions we have found helpful: (1) *Do we break such a rule in our lives?* If we do not positively model the rule, we can't expect the child to accept its validity. (2) *Do we really expect that the child can obey the rule?* If we do not believe a child is capable of adherence, we will be asking for trouble. (3) *Are we in a position to check if the rule is being followed?* If we don't have time to supervise the operation of the rule, or if we must rely on the report of other people to determine if the rule has been broken, we are encouraging deception.

3. *Hold an open discussion about the rule.* Rules require less enforcement when they have been discussed beforehand. This discussion helps the adult sell the rule; the child can be told why the rule is needed and how she or he might benefit if the rule is obeyed. Sometimes a child does not see the reason for the rule or that it can bring greater sanity and calm to a household or classroom. This discussion is also an opportunity to get the child's input on the impending rule. The child often may have ideas how the rule could be improved and made more palatable and can also be asked what help may be required to follow the rule.

4. *Prepare one or more plans if the rule is not obeyed.* This is often the crucial step. When we haven't given advance thought to the actions we might take if the rule is broken, we frequently overreact with severe punishments and hysterical screaming or underreact with mild warnings and pleas for obedience. There is a wide range of plans to consider, from rediscussing the rule to imposing appropriate penalties.

It may not be possible to undertake all four steps that are outlined here. The more of them you can incorporate, however, the greater the possibility that your rule will take hold. Parents and teachers with whom we've worked have discovered that skipping these steps makes their rules vulnerable and they must then depend on luck or fear tactics.

Don't ruin the potential effectiveness of your rules by having too many of them. A small number of quality rules goes a long way. When children can gain respect for a few rules we have, they begin to consider us as reasonable. Our subsequent expectations will be more readily accepted because children have not been thrust into power struggles.

You are now urged to go back to chapter 3 and examine the list of dos and dont's you have for children in your family or classroom. Check them against the criteria for effective rules that we have just discussed. Are the behaviors to be encouraged or discouraged clear? To both parties? Can you enforce these expectations? Have you openly discussed each one? Do you have contingency plans if you don't get what you want?

When an expectation we have is not working out well, we can often improve matters by some corrective action. For example, at one of our workshops, a kindergarten teacher was asked to identify a situation that she would like to see improved. She shared her wish that children would stop running in the classroom. Although she had stated a rule to this effect, had discussed it with the children, and made sure it was understood and its need appreciated, the running continued. We queried her as to whether she honestly believed that the children had sufficient self-control to obey the rule. She replied that there were some doubts in her mind but she wanted to persist with the rule because she was afraid an accident might occur. She did not, however, have any plan to deal with infractions except to remind the children of the rule. We created a plan together that helped the teacher beef up the rule. For three days she stopped *every* running child in his tracks and had him retravel his route, walking slowly. There were no exceptions to this action. The teacher reported that the children got less work done, but her intervention was still worth it. The running problem had practically disappeared.

Parents and teachers become drained by a stockpile of minor nuisances which accumulate because no action is taken to reduce their number. If this happens to you, you might consider taking the necessary steps to make effective rules about some of these nuisances.

BEING PERSISTENT

All too often, children hassle us because they can count on the fact that we will let them off the hook. We seldom mean to encourage children in this way. Nonetheless, children learn that what we ask of them does not have to be taken seriously whenever we explode in anger in the face of resistance and then back off with guilt and remorse, or make empty threats and then switch to pleas or bribes to change a child's mind, or go along with an unacceptable request "for this time only" and then conveniently forget our words the next time.

Besides the establishment of long-term rules, conflict can be prevented or at least contained by letting children know that we will persist with our requests or refusals, regardless of their attempts to change our mind. A persistent stance is critical to the assertive management of conflict. It communicates that we are prepared to firmly pursue our goals without having to intimidate children.

Here are some ways to be persistent with children:

The Broken Record Technique

This is a technique advocated by Manuel Smith,* one of the pioneers in assertion training. It involves calmly repeating our position again and again until the child responds to us in some acceptable way. The broken record technique is appropriate when compromise is not desirable, or we are sure what we want, or we have not been heard or adequately responded to by the child.

Examples of use of the broken record technique follow:

Parent: Gil, I want you to put away your toys now. I have to vacuum the rug (on which the toys are strewn).
Son: (No response)
Parent: (calmly) Put your toys away now.
Son: I don't wanna.
Parent: (waits a few seconds) Gil, I mean it. Put your toys away now. I am going to vacuum the rug. Let's get started.
Son: I want to keep playing.
Parent: That's good for you but not for me. Put your blocks away now and then put those books over there. (Gil starts to clean up.)

Student: Can I go get a drink of water?
Teacher: No, you can go when this lesson is over.
Student: I'm so thirsty!
Teacher: I know you're thirsty. You can get a drink as soon as the lesson is over.
Student: (pleadingly) It'll only take a minute.
Teacher: Wait until the lesson is over.

*Manuel Smith, *When I Say No, I Feel Guilty* (New York: Dial Press, 1975).

Parent: Beth, will you put the garbage outside?
Beth: (unconvincingly) Yeah, I guess so.
Parent: Beth, I want to be sure you're going to do it. Will you do it?
Beth: If I can get to it, Dad.
Parent: No, I want to know for sure one way or the other. Will you do it?
Beth: OK.

To use the broken record technique effectively, try to keep good eye contact, stand appropriately close to the child, and use a firm but relaxed voice. If a child rejects your message the first time, be careful *not to raise your voice.* (Some people are effective lowering the volume slightly with each repeated assertion.) As best as possible, avoid the impression that you are made anxious by the child's resistance.

Repeating ourselves like a broken record is much easier when a child has made a request from us rather than when we have asked something of them. With the former, we hold the power to refuse. When the situation is reversed, we must anticipate what to do if the child ultimately rebuffs us. Otherwise, the child holds all the power. For example, Gil's parent can take hold of his wrists and gently force Gil's hands to pick up some toys. Or Gil can be physically removed from the room so he no longer can play (the parent then assumes the cleaning up chore). The parent can also back off from the request and firmly say, "I was hoping you would be able to clean up the room. I'll just ask you again tomorrow." By doing this, the parent is willing to forego immediate satisfaction, but when she repeats her request the next day, Gil should feel that his mother means business.

The broken record technique does not have to be done verbally; a persistent message can be sent without talking. For example, a parent can repeatedly place, in strategic locations throughout the house, written notes reminding a child of his obligations. A teacher can likewise attach a note to a child's written work, to her desk, or to her locker/cubby. Even the simple message "no" can sometimes be communicated more forcefully by shaking your head no several times rather than saying it repeatedly.

A nonverbal approach to the broken record technique is particularly effective with young children. When a child is not willing to stay in the bedroom at night, for example, a parent can stand at the bedroom door and methodically return the wandering insomniac back to bed. This approach works well with many children as long as the parent doesn't turn the event into a silly game or a desperate struggle. The more taciturn and unruffled the parent can be, the better the technique works.

As is true with any technique, the use of the broken record method incurs some risks. It may cut off some deserved empathy for the child's position. It also seems foolish if we are not certain of our own position. Most important of all, even though it is intended to defuse anger, there is no guarantee that this technique will avoid infuriating a child. Should the child react negatively, we need to decide whether to stick to the approach regardless of the consequences. We might also try to figure out how we can be less offensive in the way we repeat ourselves.

Persistent Silence

One of the least energy-draining methods to quell a conflict is to remain silent. Silence is a very powerful behavior, yet as we have already noted, it is amazing how infrequently it is used by us parents and teachers. We assume that we must explain ourselves to children, (even when our position is already clear to them) and that we must goad them into action with words.

Waiting children out through silence works best in situations where children know what is expected of them and why. We must also be unmoved by their attempts to resist us. For example:

Jill started to watch TV while she was completing her homework even though there is a firm rule that homework must be done at the desk in her bedroom. Her mother discovered Jill's violation of the rule and said "Jill, the rule is no TV and homework at the same time. You know that." Jill responded, "Aw, come on. I can do both at once." Her mother looked at her calmly without saying a word. Jill then retorted, "Mom, you're being ridiculous!" Her mother said nothing and merely stood there waiting. Jill then pretended to occupy herself with her homework. A few minutes went by. Jill blurted out, "Mother, please leave me alone." Her mother remained impassive and silent. Jill held out a few more minutes and then went to her room.

Hearing a disturbance, a sixth-grade teacher returned to her classroom from a brief visit in the corridor with the school principal. Several children had stopped working at their desks and were chasing each other, even though the class rule is that work continues whether or not the teacher is there. The teacher got everyone's attention by silently looking from one child to the other. She then remarked, "I want you to be responsible for your own conduct. You'll never be able to do that if I have to check on you." Some children started to complain that other students egged them into the violation of the rule. Knowing that any discussion at this point would open a Pandora's box, the teacher simply stood in further silence. The children quieted down and returned to work. Later in the day, the teacher had a private discussion with the children involved in the incident. Notice that in these instances silence is not used as a way to sulk or reject children but as a tool for assertively communicating the adult position and avoiding games of manipulation.

Charting

A simple procedure for coping with a child's continuing resistance to our expectations is to chart the number of infractions and share the results with the child. Without our having to scream, nag, or use our voice much at all, charting allows us to persistently show a child how often he or she may be violating rules. Moreover, it does not require the offer of rewards or the threat of punishments.

To use this technique, begin by selecting no more than two specific behaviors you would like a child to stop. Some behaviors successfully attacked by parents and teachers with whom we have worked are: "put downs" of other children, interrupting people when talking, leaving belongings where they shouldn't be, going somewhere without adequate or proper clothing, and handing in illegible work. Ideally, choose behaviors whose slow but steady decline could be expected. Then inform the child that you will keep a record of how often that behavior occurs for a period of at least one week. Tell the child, if you wish, that you are tired of yelling all the time and would rather keep after him or her by charting. Add, "I hope this will work better also. It will if you try to cut down on (specify behavior). There won't be any rewards or punishments. Let's just see if you can cut down on (specify behavior). At the end of the week, we'll discuss how it's going."

Although charting works better if the idea is palatable to the child, you can go ahead with it even if the child disapproves of the idea. Should the child try to argue that the charting is unwarranted, invite him or her to do the charting.

The record keeping involved in charting can be done any way you like. At home, a sheet of paper can be placed on the refrigerator or the child's bedroom door with the behavior specified in writing (and pictorially for younger children), the days of the week listed, and marks entered when infractions occur. In the classroom, the paper can be located at the teacher's desk or attached to the child's desk. As an alternative, a teacher can give the child several slips of paper with his name on each and take one away for each misbehavior.

Parents and teachers report to us that they like the charting procedure because it accomplishes two things simultaneously: (1) The adult is able to be calm about the misbehavior and (2) the child becomes graphically aware of the errant behavior. In some cases, however, we have received reports that a child hassled the adult on the validity of every mark entered on the chart. When we check on the details, we often discover that the behavior to be entered was open to too much interpretation. For example, the behavior one parent had been charting was called "minding your mother." Further work by the adult in specifying the behavior to the child usually remedied the matter. It has also been helpful to suggest charting positive behaviors rather than negative behaviors. For example, one teacher was more successful recording the frequency of times a student handed in legible work than charting illegible work.

Ignoring

One of the most time-honored bits of advice from psychologists is to ignore behavior we want to discourage and attend instead to behavior we want to encourage. In psychological terms, ignoring behavior weakens its chances of recurrence. Making a fuss over it (even if we are punitive) can reinforce the behavior. This principle can be likened to the world of business: To ignore a behavior means that it gets no commercial attention; to respond to it gives the behavior free advertising.

Aware of this advice, many adults try a one-shot experiment with ignoring misbehavior. Unless the ignoring has taken the child by total surprise, a one-shot application simply doesn't work. We might even find that the behavior gets worse after initially ignoring it. Because ignoring behavior only gradually convinces children that attention will not be forthcoming, we must persist with the technique.

Ignoring is an especially appropriate response to attention-bidding actions such as clownishness, excessive dependence on adult help, and flirting. The attention seeking child who so behaves is not really interested in resisting adult authority. The behavior is continued, according to Rudolf Dreikurs,* in the mistaken belief that the adult's reaction, negative though it may be, is the child's only proof of self-worth. Nagging and coaxing are unpleasant adult behaviors, but they nonetheless satisfy a child's wish for attention and feed faulty logic that to be worthwhile means that adults must always be paying attention. Being ignored is the opposite of what the child is seeking but precisely what is needed. Of course, adults do not have to leave a child totally bereft of attention. Dreikurs advises, for example, to give the child lots of attention but only when the child is *not* seeking it.

When choosing to ignore some misbehavior, it is imperative to make the following determinations:

- *If the behavior is ignored, can tangible, harmful consequences occur before the behavior becomes sufficiently extinguished?* You would not, for example, ignore a young child playing with matches, but you can ignore almost any temper tantrum that does not involve physical abuse to the child or to others.
- *Does your way of ignoring communicate indifference or disapproval?* The surest way for ignoring to backfire is to give a child the old evil eye or storm out of the room. While it is usually impossible to be indifferent at the start, try to learn to live with the behavior that previously upset you. Give yourself a chance to build your immunity to the behavior. If it still upsets you after a few days, use a different strategy.
- *Is your attention important enough to the child that ignoring will make a difference?* You have to be careful *not* to assume that your responsiveness to a child's misbehavior is the only or even the major avenue of reinforcement. As children get

*Rudolf Dreikurs, *Children: The Challenge.* (New York: Hawthorn Books, a division of Elsevier-Dutton, 1964).

older, for example, the reinforcement (and ignoring) power of peers intensifies. If you ignore inappropriate behavior (such as alcoholic drinking), it doesn't mean your child's peers will do likewise. Also, one person's ignoring may be insufficient to counteract the attractiveness of a behavior to a child. More active forms of intervention may be needed.

DISARMING CHILDREN

The hope of every parent or teacher is to enlist children's cooperation without having to persist for a long period of time. No adult likes to be a thorn (even an assertive one) in a child's side. And who wouldn't like a swift change in a child's behavior?

It is totally unrealistic to depend on such a hope. Dealing with children usually demands some energy and persistence. There are some occasions, however, when parents or teachers can nip hassles in the bud by quickly and pleasantly disarming children. We discuss below three such methods.

Redirecting

One technique for disarming children, used frequently by parents and teachers of young children, is to redirect unacceptable behavior. Redirection is accomplished by catching children off guard and diverting their interest away from what they are doing to another activity. The key to success is the adult's ability to create a pleasurable substitute experience for the child. Sometimes the task is as simple as startling a preschooler with directions like, "Look at that pretty bird outside the window," or pretending you're a circus clown, giant monster, or a character from Sesame Street. Other times the task demands an instinctive knack for involving children in an equally absorbing activity. For example: Elaine was carpooling her son and another boy to nursery school. The boys started to fight viciously in the back seat. Elaine pulled the car over to the side of the road and said unexpectedly, "Does anyone know the name of the street we are on?" The startled boys each chimed "Johnson," the street they each live on. Elaine countered, "No, this street is Park Drive. Do you see the park over there? It's probably named Park Drive because we're driving past a park. Let's see what other streets we go on."

The boys liked hearing and repeating the new street names with every turn of the car. They also learned that a street could be several blocks long. The fighting ceased. (Elaine repeated this activity every day for a week and the boys had a great time memorizing the route to school.)

As adults who try to redirect can attest, redirection doesn't always work. There are times when a child is very stubborn about the thing she is into and will not be diverted to a new interest. In that case, there is still the possibility of making subtle shifts in the experience while still maintaining the child's preoccupation. Here is an example: Out of the clear, blue sky, Tracy asked her nursery teacher if the class could have a Halloween party that day (it was one month after Halloween). When informed that Halloween did not return until the following October, Tracy began to sob uncontrollably and refused to accept the teacher's information. Thinking quickly, the teacher gathered a small group of children around Tracy and started to ask each of them to recall the costumes worn by their classmates when Halloween was last celebrated. In a matter of minutes, Tracy and the other children were relishing memories of the past Halloween experience and started to discuss plans for next year's costumes. Tracy never mentioned her wish for a Halloween party again.

Some parents and teachers complain that redirecting spoils children by indulging a child's every whim. Our belief is that redirection is best suited for those situations when it simply isn't worth a whole lot of fuss to deal with a child. Care should be taken, however, to avoid designating nearly every potential hassle as not worth it. Redirecting too often will only reinforce a child's engaging in the very behavior we wish would be avoided.

We might also point out that redirecting can be helpful with older children. Of course, their behavior is not as easily diverted as is a younger child's, but we can still seek to change the course of their behavior by appealing to other needs. This idea can be especially attractive to teachers as a vehicle for enhancing thinking and learning. For example, we have witnessed teachers who dealt with a forbidden game of craps in the back of a classroom by interesting the culprits in the mathematical probability of various combinations of dice; enticed a group of children into learning how to tape record a "dirty" song they composed; and responded to silly verbal insults that students were hurling at each other by challenging them to find more sophisticated words of insult in a dictionary.

Parents can sometimes use redirection to defuse a child's stubbornness. For example, one parent we know finally got her teenager to play records less loudly by initiating a conversation with her about the rock groups being played. To hear her mother, the daughter lowered the volume without realizing it. A few minutes later, the girl smiled at the realization of what she had done to accommodate her mother. They both laughed. After that, the daughter was more considerate.

Doing the Opposite

A second way to disarm children is to do or say the opposite of what a child expects of us. For example, we could go along suddenly with a request we have steadfastly refused, approve of immature behavior, give surprising advice, or even encourage a child to give up his efforts to please us. When we do such unexpected things we are, in effect, taking our sails out of the child's wind. Even if he once delighted in pushing us around, we can now remove ourselves as objects of battle and allow the child to make a clearer decision about how he wants to act.

This idea is akin to the notion of reverse psychology. Adults often tell us, "If I say A, my child will just do B. I'd be better off starting with the opposite of what I want." Despite their belief in reverse psychology, however, few adults we meet ever attempt it. Some fear that the strategy will boomerang, others are concerned that the tactic is manipulative and dishonest; still others are unwilling to give up direct confrontation.

Doing the opposite of what children expect works best if our goal is to show them, in a subtle way, that they have the power to choose a different course of action. It is not a strategy to pull the wool over their eyes and show them that they can be outwitted, but a loving, good-natured way to help children change their behavior. Children, from toddlers to adolescents, are often trapped by the illusion that stubborn resistance or negative acting out is the only avenue of self-determination. Doing the opposite is a technique geared toward helping children discover that they have the power to assert themselves positively, as an alternative to the negative power of stubborn resistance. Here are some illustrations: Ellen and Bob are fond of taking long walks on the weekend. Their five-year-old daughter, Nancy, usually wants to accompany them but invariably asks to be carried along the way. Usually Ellen and Bob are annoyed by this request and beg Nancy to try to walk by herself. Nancy gets her way, though, after a lot of whining and sit-down strikes. One day when the usual resistance occurred, Ellen said, "You know, Nancy, you really may become tired walking by yourself. We'll carry you." Ellen said this message matter of factly, with no hint of being derogatory. As she had hoped, Nancy was intrigued by her mother's remarks and said, "No, I can make it home."

Whenever it was nap time at the day care center, three-year-old Billy always refused to nap, despite the fact that he was consistently tired and cranky by the afternoon. Active attempts to persuade Billy never worked, so the adult in charge decided to handle his resistance differently. One day she went over to Billy and said pleasantly, "It's time for a nap." Predictably, Billy countered, "I don't wanna." Unpredictably, the adult said, "OK" and did nothing further. A few minutes later, Billy came over to her and repeated, "I don't wanna take a nap." The adult responded again, "You don't have to." A few more minutes passed and then Billy took his blanket from his cubby and climbed on a cot for a long nap.

A ninth grader, Jill, was asked out on a date by Joe, a high school senior with a wild reputation. She was personally hesitant to get involved with him but was attracted to accept the date as a way to upset her parents, whom she considers old-fashioned. Approaching her father, she blurted out, "Will you let me go on a date with Joe? I don't see why I can't but I bet you won't let me!" Father was stunned for a few seconds by her sudden charge and pondered what to say. Collecting his thoughts, he responded softly, "You know, Jill, I guess going on a date with that boy would be exciting. You'd feel pretty grown up. I'll think about it and we'll talk it over tonight. I have to go out now." Totally unprepared for these remarks, Jill stopped still in her tracks as her father left the house. She then realized how ridiculous her behavior had been and that she would find a date with Joe more scary than exciting. She later told her father she had changed her mind about the date.

In each of these situations, the child's power to defy, upset, or annoy the adult was accepted rather than blocked. Accepting the child's resistance allowed several things to happen: The adult got the child's full attention; the child's satisfaction with being able to hassle an adult was lessened; the immaturity of the child's behavior became evident to the child; and the child was challenged to take charge of himself.

Doing the opposite of what a child expects does not work all the time either. Nancy might have readily accepted her parents' willingness to carry her; Billy might have been cranky all afternoon; Jill might have agreed that a date with Joe would be exciting. Understandably, then, this strategy is not appropriate for those situations in which we need immediate compliance. We must allow for the possibility of coming away unsatisfied from the encounter. However, even if we lose initially, a child just may change his mind later on because we have given him the control to do so.

When you experiment with doing the opposite, bear in mind these hints:

- Try it initially in a situation which involves a relatively minor conflict and see how it feels and works.
- Leave yourself an "out" if you are worried about what the child will do (Jill's father did this).
- Use humor (but avoid sarcasm).
- Think about what you can say that would be startling and challenging to the child.

Making Our Expectations Attractive

A third possibility for disarming children is to make it attractive to comply with our wishes. Cooperation can often be enlisted if fringe benefits are involved for the child.

From the outset, it needs to be very clear that we are not talking about promising a child a reward in frantic reaction to his disobedience.* When we are at wit's end, the worst thing to do is to bribe a child—bribery then becomes an invitation to manipulate us.

Psychologists typically classify rewards into two categories: *tangible reinforcers* and *social reinforcers*. The former involves giving pleasurable items (such as food treats, money, and toys), privileges (like staying up late, no homework, extra recess), or

---

*We are reminded of a balloon hawker at a Thanksgiving parade who appealed to this sense of urgency by chanting, "If you cry, your mother will buy."

permission for any activity the child especially likes. These rewards can be given outright or points can be accumulated in order to win the right to the reward.

The whole business of tangible rewards has brought considerable debate. Some psychologists and educators abhor the idea while others find any objection to it hypocritical. Adults, they argue, do things for rewards like money. Why can't children?

Our view is that tangible rewards are appropriate options when children are expected to do things which are very difficult, anxiety provoking, or unappealing. Essentially, adults have to determine whether the means (tangible rewards) justify the end. If the behavior in question is important for the well-being of the family (such as cleaning the house and doing the laundry), or enhances the self-esteem of the child (such as helping him learn the habit of finishing a job completely), the end may very well justify the use of tangible rewards. Our disclaimer is that tangible rewards are only effective in helping a child get started in the right direction. They do not bring permanent results, let alone inner-direction and self-discipline. Furthermore, rewards cannot be constant. Adults who over-reward tend to be faced with a child who resists or feels rejected if a treat is not forthcoming.

A fourth-grade teacher we know has used tangible rewards in a very sensible manner. From her past teaching experience, she has found that nine-year-olds have trouble being consistently prepared and organized for all their assignments (in earlier grades, they are not expected to handle outside work). Rather than waiting till the problem is at hand, she disarms her students in September by announcing that each of them will receive a "sunshine telegram" congratulating the student for every week in which he or she is prepared 100 percent of the time. The children are also informed that for every five telegrams they each accumulate, a special treat is granted. Fifteen telegrams, for example, bring an invitation to go for an ice cream cone with the teacher during lunch hour. The students are very responsive to this incentive system and develop considerable pride by learning good habits of preparation. There are enough opportunities for everyone to get some treats and the children have agreed not to put down classmates who lag behind in telegrams. The teacher also finds that the effort involved for her in keeping records on the children and arranging for the treats, although time consuming, demands less energy than the hassles she previously had to endure with unprepared students. In this situation, the end certainly justifies the means.

Social reinforcers include such responses as appreciation, praise, attention, smiling, and embraces. They are used most commonly as an accompaniment to behavior we desire from a child. Sometimes merely beginning a request with words like, "I'd sure like it if . . ." and, "I would really appreciate it if . . ." enlist cooperation. Keeping pleasant company with children while they clean their room or when they are getting ready for bed is also reinforcing. Giving compliments or thanks after a child has been cooperative helps to show our goodwill. Any of these social reinforcers can best disarm and win over a child when they are given in situations where we have previously acted exasperated or have taken the child's cooperation for granted. We must remember, though, to initiate social reinforcers when we feel under control. We should never reinforce a child in desperation or after we have already been put through the wringer.

Finally, every parent or teacher needs to understand the importance of reinforcing the small steps a child takes in the direction of accomplishing a big, complex task. So often, when a child is not doing what we hope for, the first tendency is to bear down on the failures. Usually, if we look hard enough, we can catch positive behaviors to compliment which, if nurtured, will bring about the overall result we are seeking For example:

A mother used to berate her young child's clumsy pouring of juice. One day, she decided to praise every small step the child took in pouring. "Bring the pitcher right next to the glass. Good. Hold the pitcher with two hands. Great! Now pour a tiny bit to see if it will work. Yeh, it does. Good work. OK, you can pour the juice in the glass to just before the top. Fine! Good for you!"

A teacher dealt with a second-grade student who took a long time getting to work on his math by saying, "I'm glad you are sitting quietly and have your pencil ready. You are ready to work."

A father was constantly after his eleven-year-old son to fold his clothes correctly. One day when he noted some slight improvement, he offered, "Thanks for trying to fold your shirts instead of rolling them up in a ball. Will you let me teach you again how to fold your clothes so that you get even fewer wrinkles?"

COMPROMISE OR PENALIZE?

We hope by now that you are impressed by the number of alternate ways to cope with unacceptable behavior in children.* When all else fails, however, resolving hassles sometimes comes down to an either–or choice—either compromise or penalize. Unless we work out some bargain with children or let them experience unpleasant consequences for their actions, the hassle between us could continue *ad infinitum*.

The choice between compromising and penalizing is exceedingly difficult. We must consider a myriad of factors such as the child's physical and psychological readiness to meet our demands; the time needed to work out a compromise or enforce a penalty; and the learning we hope the child gleans from the situation. We might, for example, compromise on our expectation that a four-year-old clean up *all* the toys strewn about the room if the child is somewhat overwhelmed by the task. We could also determine that the time spent keeping a child after school punishes us more than the child. But we might decide to impose a penalty if we want a child to learn that our expectation to return home on time is non-negotiable.

The only recommendation we can stand unequivocally behind is to be sure that you incorporate both compromises and penalties into your approach to children. *If you are exclusively a compromiser, children will surely take advantage of you. If you are exclusively a penalizer, children will become immune to your authority.* As we will discuss in chapter 7, the need for compromise is particularly important as children get older and the necessity of external control diminishes. It is also important not to vacillate between compromising and penalizing to resolve a specific conflict. You don't negotiate a bedtime one night and threaten punishment the next. Children respond best to consistency.

Compromise is often avoided even though it should be a natural part of life. No one, not even adults, can get what they want all the time. Besides, always sticking to our guns is not necessarily the highest virtue in managing children. It can at times increase conflict if the children really want to stick to their guns as well.

*You will find a more comprehensive listing of alternate strategies in *How to Influence Children* (New York: Van Nostrand Reinhold, 1978) by Charles Schaefer.

As long as our attitude about the necessity for occasional compromise is positive, it is unlikely that an offer to work out an agreeable arrangement with children will feel weak to either party.

In the Smith household, for example, both parents work. Because they are quite tired when they get home at dinnertime, they expect their sons, ages 11 and 13, to set the dinner table and clean the kitchen after dinner is over. (The cooking is left to the parents.) The Smith children are adamantly opposed to this arrangement, claiming that they are as tired from school as their parents are from work and that they get all the scut work while the parents have the enjoyment of cooking. The Smiths don't accept that their sons are so tired and also insist that letting the boys cook will create more trouble for them than it is worth. After several weeks of argument and unwashed dishes, the parents decide to eliminate the boys' allowance as a penalty for shirking their responsibilities. The threatened penalty works to some degree except that now the boys, previously united in their stand against the parents, bicker nightly over who is not doing his proper share of the work. Their performance on other household chores also slackens. The Smiths are left with a situation in which none of their needs are really being met. But they are afraid to change their stand lest their parental authority becomes further undermined.

The Smiths' fear, in our opinion, is unfounded. While it is true that parents should often persist with their expectations even when they are unpopular, the Smiths must also realize that parents can not have total control over their children's actions unless they are willing to run their home like a boot camp. If they are able to recognize how much the entire situation has gotten out of hand, it should be possible for them to accept the stalemate for what it is—not a *defeat*, but a reality that both they and their children share. They can then discuss the stalemated conflict in a straightforward, nondefensive way with their sons and work out a compromise. For example, the parents might agree to relieve the boys of some other responsibilities to encourage acceptance of their dinnertime chores.

Some adults are even more reluctant to penalize than others are to compromise. They fail to accept that children need external controls to comply with adult expectations. (In fact, rather than wishing adults would always leave them alone, children want to know that they can rely on adults to control them when they cannot control themselves.) Moreover, these adults forget that penalties are a component of any system of social order. If we drive above the speed limit, we may get a ticket. If we fail to pay our income tax on time, we have to pay interest on the amount due. If we are absent from work more than the number of permitted days, our pay is docked. Why can't a child who continually kicks a sibling or classmate be put in "solitary confinement" for a few hours?

In fact, we recently met a mother who was faced with the problem of a four-year-old kicking his two-year-old brother. She believed that the older child would resent his younger brother even more if he received any serious penalty. Therefore, she decided that it was better to deal with the situation with soft-spoken verbal reprimands. Because she overexaggerated the negative effects of penalties, the mother simply wasn't doing her job as protector of her two-year-old's rights.

We believe that compromising is not necessarily a sign of weakness and penalizing is not necessarily an indication of meanness. Both are legitimately different ways to help a child satisfy adult expectations. A compromiser is being weak if he wants only to appease or win favor; a penalizer is being mean if he imposes penalties only to seek retaliation.

The Assertive Compromiser

When we decide to compromise with a child, we must be careful not to *panic* or *deceive*. Adults who panic usually wind up making deals in which they feel like losers. Adults who deceive make deals in which children are tricked into believing they are winners. To avoid these errors, the adult who is an assertive compromiser needs to do two things at once: (1) Stay in personal control of the situation by being very clear about what she or he is willing to do and not to do, and (2) be sure that the offer to compromise is sincere.

It also helps to be prepared with several options for compromise. Often, adults do not realize how many ways they can approach compromise. Here are some alternatives:

1. *Give a choice about how or when or where an expectation is enforced.* Although we may not be willing to retreat from our demand, we can negotiate when it must be fulfilled, how it is to be accomplished, where it is to be done, or what happens if we are

not satisfied. For example, though we may insist that a child's room be cleaned, we can negotiate the time by which it has to be done, how "clean" is clean, and which of two penalties the child prefers if he forgets to do it.

2. *Say no to a request but provide alternatives.* We may be totally rejecting of a request made by a child but can still suggest some ideas to satisfy his or her needs. For example, a student might ask a teacher if class could be held outdoors because it is a warm, sunny day. The teacher can reject the request but offer a longer outdoor recess.

3. *Make an exchange.* If your twelve-year-old son refuses to perform a certain task, you can ask him if he would be willing to change his mind in exchange for canceling or postponing some other responsibility. For example, a child who balks at shoveling six inches of snow from the front sidewalk can be excused from walking the dog for the remainder of the week.

4. *Meet children half-way.* In a conflict situation where both adults and children have legitimate rights, a compromise can be arranged in which each party gets some but not all of their needs met. For example, if both parents and their children like to make active use of the telephone during the evening, the children could be given telephone rights from 7:00 to 8:30 and the parents from 8:30 to 10:00.

5. *Ask the child to suggest a solution.* Adults often assume that they must make the first offer. Sometimes asking a child for a solution to a conflict is preferable. A child may even be willing to give more ground than we expect if given the opportunity to make a suggestion. For example, a teacher and a student were involved in a dispute over the neatness of a homework assignment. When the student was asked how the dispute could be resolved, he offered to recopy the assignment as long as he didn't miss any time from lunch or recess. The teacher happily agreed.

6. *Jointly look for a mutual solution.* When time permits, it is especially helpful to sit down with a willing child and draw up a list of several tentative solutions to a conflict. It is crucial to explain to the child that nothing on the list (neither what you nor the child contributes) is binding. The purpose of the list is simply to identify all the alternate solutions that may exist for a problem. A discussion can then be held to figure out what solution might best satisfy both adult and child. For example, a father wanted his son to stop ridiculing his younger sister, but the son insisted that

the ridiculing didn't bother the sister. After a problem-solving discussion, they mutually agreed that the father could give his son an unobstrusive hand signal when the father thought the ridicule was excessive. Otherwise, he could not intervene. In this solution, the father was satisfied that he could have some influence with his son, and at the same time, the son did not feel that the father was overly intrusive.

The Assertive Penalizer

The assertive way to approach penalty giving is to view ourselves as something of an umpire or referee. In a competitive game, the officials assess penalties for a group of infractions which have already been specified. The penalties themselves are well known in advance of the infractions and are usually administered impersonally, yet immediately. They are also suited to the seriousness of the infraction. (For example, in football, there is a fifteen-yard penalty for holding, but only a five-yard penalty for being offside.) Finally, they are logically fitted to the circumstances of the game; the other team gains an advantage if we don't play by the rules.

Our outlook is just the opposite of a referee's when we feel upset over *having* to penalize a child to change behavior. In our annoyance we angrily dish out penalties as opposed to quickly administering them. Furthermore, we may see the misdeed as a personal affront rather than a "game infraction." As a result, the doer is chastised rather than the misdeed. Instead of learning to control the misdeed in the future, the child merely learns to resent adult authority.

The penalties themselves often come by surprise and are ill-conceived. They seldom are logically related to or commensurate with the "crime"; our first instinct is to erupt with, "Go to your room for the rest of the day!" or, "No TV for a week," without any prior reflection as to whether such penalties make sense and are fair. Consequently, we rarely have a leg to stand on when a child disputes our decision.

To help develop an assertive approach to penalty giving, we can try following these guidelines and suggestions:

1. *Ask ourselves if it is possible to do nothing at all.* Among the most powerful and reasonable penalties is to allow a child to experience the natural consequences of his actions. For example:

- If we set food on the dinner table at a pre-established time, a child's food will get cold if he is not there to eat it.
- If we are willing to wash dirty clothes placed only in a hamper, clothes left elsewhere will go unwashed.
- If we teach a lesson with the assumption that all children are prepared, an unprepared child will be confused.
- If a child can't get ready in the morning and he misses the bus, he will have to walk to school or stay home.
- If a student forgets to bring money or a permission slip for a class trip, he will have to stay in another classroom for the day.

As long as the natural consequence is sufficiently unpleasant to children (without being dangerous), they often will learn for themselves not to act that way again.

2. *The more often we try to fit the penalty to the misdeed, the better we get at it.* When a situation is devoid of effective natural consequences, the penalty we establish needs to be relevant for a child to best appreciate its validity. Fitting a penalty to a misdeed is an art which takes practice.* In our initial attempts, we need to ask ourselves what penalty can be imposed which will emphasize the misbehavior rather than the naughtiness of the misbehaver. Examples are:

- If students persist in passing notes in class, we might promise to read the notes aloud.
- If a child suddenly won't eat the brand of cereal he begged us to buy, we refuse to buy another brand until the current one is finished.
- If a student loses her list of spelling words more than once, she is required to make a duplicate list (one for home and one for school) for a few weeks.
- If children are rowdy at the dinner table, we arrange for them to eat in separate rooms.

3. *Let children decide between obedience and receiving a penalty.* Because we want children to take responsibility for their own behavior, it is preferable to give them the choice of obedience or penalty as much as we can. So when we catch them in the middle of an unacceptable act, we can tell them pleasantly, "Look, you have a choice. You can either stop that or [penalty]. You decide."

*For guidance see Rudolf Driekurs and Pearl Cassel, *Discipline Without Tears* (New York: Hawthorn Books, A Division of Elsevier-Dutton, 1972).

If they persist with the behavior in question, we should look at it as if they are implicitly choosing the penalty, accept their decision with respect, and carry it out. For example, a teacher might say to a student who is found copying a classmate's work, "I don't think you'll learn anything from copying. You can choose to do your own work now or I will change your seat to the back of the room. Which do you want?" If the student indicates by his subsequent behavior that he wants his seat moved, the teacher can do so without adverse comments.

4. *One of the most meaningful penalties is to ask children to figure out a plan for changing their behavior.* Whenever possible, we can tell misbehaving children that we expect them to suggest a way they can help themselves change their behavior. We need to explain, however, that we do not want a simple promise, but a clear indication of what they will do to counteract the present misbehavior. For example, a child who continually interrupts other students during class discussion might propose that she sit next to the teacher as a reminder not to interrupt the next discussion. If the child refuses to suggest a plan at all, she can be assigned to some boring place of our choice (such as a bathroom, a hallway, or a bench in the back of a room) until the child comes up with a plan. When the plan is presented and agreed to by the parent or teacher, the child is expected to keep to the plan. If the child doesn't, or for some reason the plan doesn't work, the child is then asked to submit a new plan. This approach requires some sophistication, so it is important to teach a child what is meant by a plan and to give some initial help in formulating one.*

5. *Maintain a few standard penalties that can be used as standbys in case more logical consequences are not available.* The best standard penalties deprive children of some pleasurable activity such as watching TV, playing with friends, riding bicycles, going outside during recess or lunch, or attending a special event. It is important that equally pleasurable experiences are not available at the time children are being penalized. One way to ensure this is to use some form of social isolation, (see number four, above). During early childhood, a procedure called "time out" can be effective. It involves placing

*See William Glasser, *Schools Without Failure* (New York: Harper & Row, 1969) and William Glasser, *Reality Therapy* (New York: Harper & Row, 1965) for further discussion of this idea.

the child in a boring place for a short period of time (research studies have shown that three minutes of time out work as well as thirty minutes) *every time the child engages in a specific behavior we want to stop.* The procedure does not work, however, if we are harsh or preaching as we carry it out; if we let a child play with toys or be otherwise entertained; if we do it for more than one behavior at a time; if we fail to add additional minutes for refusals to go to time out, or for destructive behavior during it; or if we forget to praise a child for doing time out well. Naturally, we must also explain and demonstrate the procedure and its rules when we use it for the first time.*

6. *Use physical force to control behavior that must be stopped immediately.* Although spanking and other forms of corporal punishment create more problems than they may cure, there is no reason to shy away from active physical restraint when a child's behavior is very much out of bounds. If our child hits us, for example, we should immediately move behind him and lock our arms around his, emphatically adding that hitting will not be tolerated. Our grip should not be relaxed until we determine that we have provided sufficient control, not when a child kicks up too much of a fuss. One method is to immediately tell the child that we will hold him for thirty seconds or one minute and then start counting. Similarly, cupping our hand over the mouth of a hysterically screaming child can be effective so long as we do it for no more than five seconds at a time and assure the child that we will not harm him. Providing physical restraint when a child has gone berserk is an important gift. He can always count on our physical strength when it is needed.

7. *Don't give in or argue with children who beg to be saved from a penalty.* When we impose a penalty, we can usually count on children to try to talk us out of it. Suddenly, promises to be good are uttered, protests that we are unfair ring out, or offers to bargain with us abound. We must kindly and firmly follow through with the penalty at this point, making no attempt to convince the children that we are just and that they deserve what is coming to them. Nor should we assuage our guilt with comments that we hate doing this to them.

*See Gerald R. Patterson, *Living With Children* (Revised), (Champaign, Ill.: Research Press, 1976), for more information about time out.

EXPERIMENTATION PAYS OFF—TO A POINT

Given the wide range of ways to avoid power struggles and influence children's behavior, it makes sense to experiment with as many of them as possible before choosing those that help you the most. Too often we get locked into the same way of doing things and thus, trying out new approaches can bring a breath of fresh air.

As you experiment, make some informal notes as to which approaches work best in which situations. Be careful, however, not to rush the period of experimentation. We have heard accounts of parents or teachers who bombarded their children with five to ten new discipline techniques within a day or two. Pick the appropriate spots to introduce changes in how you deal with conflict. Likewise, don't experiment on a one-shot basis. Try an approach a few times to see if you like it and have confidence in it. Also, if you reject a method, try it again a week or month later. It may suit you, the child, and the situation better at that time.

If, after sufficient experimentation, you find several approaches that work for you, don't flip-flop from one to the other as you discipline a particular child. Settling on three or four relatively permanent approaches helps a child experience you as both consistent and flexible.

7 | As Children Grow

'I'he seasons of the year recur; history repeats itself, and styles of yesteryear return, but the ways we deal with children do not remain the same year after year. As children grow physically, intellectually, psychologically, and ethically, they require—and often demand—that we change how we treat them.

Despite our acceptance of this phenomenon, we may still be confused about how to adjust our authority role to these developmental changes. At this juncture in the book, we think it would be helpful to briefly examine this confusion and, at the same time, identify those assertive skills we have discussed in previous chapters which deserve special consideration at particular points in the developmental life of a child.

At the outset, it is important to remind ourselves that children do not develop at the same rate. All eighteen-month-olds, for example, are not walking and all fourteen-year-olds are not interested in the opposite sex. Moreover, different family systems, different sibling positions, and different schools, neighborhoods, and peers all affect a child's development. So a discussion such as the one which follows will, perforce, contain generalizations which may not completely reflect the idiosyncracies of your children or the special circumstances of their life.

BIRTH TO TWO—THE BEGINNINGS OF SELF

Children do not enter the world all alike. Some infants are calm and bubbly, some are tense and cranky, and some active and strong-willed. There are babies who keep to a schedule and ones who are totally unpredictable. Some have ravenous appetites; others are contented with a few ounces of milk.

The first year of life is the time for parents to become acquainted with the unique behavior patterns of their newborn. It is also a time of incredible give and take. Sometimes it is the infant who is leading and the parents who are following. Other times the roles of leader and follower are totally reversed. This is as it should be. Babies teach us how to get along with them and we teach babies how to get along with us.

Even though infants are utterly dependent on their parents, they still wield considerable power. The capacity of infants to control our lives can be very unsettling. Who else can get adults to change their entire pattern of activity and sleep? We can worry even at this earliest stage in a child's life that the baby is getting the upper hand in the relationship. Will picking the child up every time she cries set a dangerous precedent for how we respond to future requests? Will letting the infant nurse continuously make him a tyrant when he reaches toddlerhood? Too often, a premature panic sets in. But it is really too soon for parents to be concerned about whether they are strict enough. This is the time to give to a child; it is not the time to actively demand or deny.

We do not mean to imply that parents must do whatever an infant seemingly demands of them. That stance would surely wear parents out completely and interfere with other needs they have. What is suggested here is to adopt the attitude that the first months are rightfully set aside to provide for the baby *to the extent that our hearts and bodies are willing.* If we are not in a good mood or are especially fatigued, a baby can be left to cry. We should not provide out of guilt, however. It is best to start training ourselves from the beginning to act from positive motivations rather than negative ones.

At birth the infant's sensitivity to touch and sound are the most well developed; visual ability follows closely. The real struggle for infants is to learn to *use* their senses and their bodies. As muscular maturation occurs, babies develop new ways to manipulate their hands, mouth, feet, and teeth. This behavior sets the stage for crawling, grasping, biting, walking, and talking. Indeed, the only way very young children learn about the objects and people around them is through sensory-motor activity.

Because the child's primary way of making contact with the world is physical, adult responses to the child should be physical as well. Touching of all types demonstrates our caring: cuddling, holding, dressing, washing, and other activities are all ways to develop a relationship with a very young child. Patient touching and holding are also the best ways to restrain an infant when she is fussing. Talking is fine, too, as long as it is soothing. Singing can be used as an alternate strategy to comfort a newborn.

During the first year of life and into the second, physical experimentation is so important to a child's total development that we need to do everything possible to support it. In particular, we should encourage, within safe limits, kicking, biting, and any move to sit up, stand, or turn over. Parents can become overprotective and fearful especially when a child is beginning to crawl, or walk, and parents may rely too heavily on playpens (which bore children and inhibit exploration) to avoid harm. It is better to use playpens sparingly and take the time to make the house as safe as possible for the child's exploration by removing sharp, fragile, or small objects.

As infants become toddlers, discipline becomes a genuine issue. Toddlers get into things, and can't discriminate what is acceptable to adults and what is not. Also, their understanding is inhibited because of their limited verbal skills. Clear limits about what they can touch are necessary. The best approach to discipline for toddlers is brief, firm statements and physical restraint. If the child is doing something that we want to stop, it is best to say no and name the object involved (such as, "no—dishes") and, if that does not suffice, to remove the child from the situation. (Slaps on the hand may prove an effective deterrent but often make children anxious and irritable.) At this age, diversion is also helpful. When we distract children from what they are doing and get them to do something more acceptable to us, we avoid unnecessary conflicts.

The key to discipline with toddlers is to follow through. We shouldn't say no and then fail to remove, restrain, or redirect them if the behavior continues. Inconsistent discipline will only lead to larger problems later on. Being firm with little children not only helps them to learn what is expected of them but also gives them a sense of security. They know that there is someone in their environment who will keep them safe, love them, and be strong for them.

One piece of advice should be added. It is fruitless to think we can always stop toddlers from continuing a behavior which is totally under their control. Staying awake, refusing to eat, and crying are good examples. We are much better off asserting ourselves in areas where we control matters.

By age one, for example, a child, no matter how problematic his infancy, should not have to be rocked to sleep in his parents' arms. The child's protestations with being put to bed at a designated time cannot be stopped, but the parents are certainly able, *if they so choose,* to ignore the crying or refuse to run back into the room several times to make sure a pacifier is available. Even if a child is able to climb out of a crib, he can be returned as often as necessary to learn that his parents can enforce certain limits.

TWO TO SIX—THE EMERGENT SELF

During this period a child's development becomes more complex and more rapid. For the child, exploring, learning new skills, and developing a sense of self and of others are exciting tasks to accomplish. For the adult, these years can be difficult because so many things happen simultaneously.

As in infancy, physical development is still extremely important in this age group, especially for children from two to four years old. Touching objects and people, walking, running, jumping, falling, and spilling are just some of the physical activities that young children consider fascinating and engage in with delight. These behaviors are repeated again and again—much to adult dismay—and often are mistaken for misbehavior or hyperactivity. Repeating physical actions, however, produces a sense of competence in children. They think a lot with their bodies.

Children will appear clumsy and distractable at this stage. Coarse physical movements develop first. More difficult skills such as manipulating eating utensils, coloring within the lines, holding a glass, or buttoning a shirt are much harder to accomplish and only begin to emerge at the end of this stage. Children's distractibility is also natural. Their attention moves from one focus to another quickly. No sooner do they begin to play with one toy than another toy looks more attractive. Their eagerness to explore and to learn is overwhelming and their energy seems endless.

From the adult side, the result is a messy house or classroom, noise, broken dishes, dirty clothes, and screeching cats. It often feels like a game of "last one standing." Will the child or the adult drop from exhaustion first?

Children are also trying to understand their world, and their emergent ability to talk helps them to do this. Children are busy identifying the names of things, learning to put words together and, as a result, thinking and questioning. Their mental energy is as boundless as their physical energy. They are filled with questions and, seemingly, can't wait for answers. "What's this?" and "Why?" are asked over and over again. In the same way that physical actions are repeated until the child feels a sense of mastery, words and questions are repeated until the child gains both the ability to use the words and an understanding of their meanings.

Early childhood also begins the process of identity formation. "Where do I stop and others begin? Who am I? How am I different from other things and other people?" These questions, although not stated in sophisticated terms, are of great concern to young children. In the first years of this stage, children begin to realize that children and adults are not extensions of each other but separate persons. This is both exciting and frightening. Very young children can often be seen running away from a parent and quickly running back to them. Their emergent sense of self sparks both need for independence and a fear of loss of security. This conflict manifests itself in many ways. For example, a child may say. "I can do it," and then "You do it for me"; or "I want to go," and then add, "Don't leave me."

Choice has become real for the child. A two-year-old child, for example, can now say "no" to a parent. He can say "mine." He can fight back, kick, and scream to get his way. As a person with wishes and needs, he is the center of his world and believes everyone should cater to him. This egocentric behavior is a natural part of a child's growth.

Luckily, a sense of obedience, of conscience, and of responsibility do begin to emerge. Although these concepts are not well developed, children have the capacity to learn what's acceptable and unacceptable and to realize that there are other people in the world to consider. By about age three, for instance, children are becoming sincerely interested in other children who are not seen solely as rivals for adult attention but as sources of learning and companionship. But the young child's grasp of acceptable interpersonal behavior is tentative, and conflict exists between wanting to be cooperative and competitive with peers.

The critical tasks for adults whose children are at this stage of development are encouragement of *independent actions* and appropriate *limit setting*.

Everything that we can do to increase self-reliance aids a child to become less egocentric. Children remain egocentric precisely because they are dependent on adults. When the child develops new skills that decrease dependence on adult help, a firmer and more positive sense of self emerges. In turn, a more heightened sense of self leads to a clearer understanding of the viewpoints and needs of others.

Adults often resist the teaching of self-reliant skills as much as children resist learning them. It's easier, it's less time consuming, and above all, it feels kinder to give in to a child's dependencies than to encourage self-reliant behavior. When Luke was two, for example, his parents liked to take walks and bring him along in a stroller. Every time Luke wanted to get out of his stroller, he was discouraged. His parents did not want to slow down the walk or have it interrupted by Luke's determination to push the stroller himself. By the time Luke was four, he became so accustomed to riding in his stroller that whenever his parents wished him to go by foot, he refused. They tried to reason with Luke that he was old enough to give up the stroller, but to no avail. When a friend suggested that the stroller be given away, Luke's parents were quite resistant, believing it would be cruel of them to do that. The point to all this is that when strollers (and bottles, cribs, and the like) are no longer needed, even if we failed to encourage earlier efforts toward self-reliance, it is probably a gift to the child to give them away.

Limit setting, on the other hand, should be contingent on the child's ability to do what is being required. For example, young children are sometimes expected to wait quietly and sit still in a department store or a supermarket while all around them are interesting objects and a challenging maze of aisles and intersections. In order to enforce such a difficult expectation, the adult usually has to threaten, intimidate, spank, or bribe. The only way such measures can be avoided is for adults to involve the child in the shopping or provide something for the child to play with.

At the same time, we do not have to shy away from setting rules which a child is capable of following. For example, even though physical activity is essential, where, how, and with what objects children play at home or in school can be delineated. Rules can be set about how a young child behaves at the dinner table, what clothes to wear for a visit to grandparents, what snacks can be eaten between meals, when bedtime occurs, and how belongings are treated. The rules we have, however, need to be stated and restated until they are internalized. Beginning statements over and over again with the simple phrase, "The rule is. . . ." helps a child focus on what we are saying. It is also important to show young children what we expect, not just tell them. And this is a good time to start accompanying directives with brief, understandable reasons, such as, "Push your cup away from the edge of the table. The juice won't spill if you do that." By doing this a child begins to sense that our authority is more rational than arbitrary.

Even if we make appropriate demands, a preschooler will frequently not listen to us. As we have noted, resistance for its own sake is natural at this stage. The child wants to feel independent, and may not do something just to feel that she has the power to stand up to adults. Although this display of strength is important to the child, the ability of adults to control the child is equally critical. If adults consistently fail to impose their authority against a child's will, the child can not be assured that the parent has the power to protect her. *The ability to both gratify a child's needs and wishes and to withhold gratification legitimates adult authority in the mind of a young child.* Only in the later stages of development does a child really understand the role of adult authority.

At first glance, the need for both child and adult to be strong presents a tricky issue. Children do need to get their way sometimes to gain self-esteem. But if the resistance occurs in an area where a responsible adult judges that the child must comply, who should win? We feel it must be the adult who emerges victorious. Standing our ground on important issues satisfies our needs, and benefits the child by requiring responsibility and the development of a social consciousness.

Recognizing the need to stand our ground on important issues, we must make every effort to discourage power struggles. Typically, young children are enticed into power struggles when adults are indecisive. If they sense that we are unsure of ourselves (a clear sign is when we talk too much), they gain considerable leverage. Therefore, when we have a non-negotiable expectation, we should quietly proceed to carry out whatever action is needed. If a child's bedtime is eight o'clock, he needs to be carried up to bed in the event he will not go willingly. Or if Mommy or Daddy must leave to go to work in the morning, they can give a brief goodbye kiss at the front door of the house or upon arrival at the day care center, but then promptly depart. Coaxing a child into accepting these necessities usually increases resistance. Whatever protests occur can instead be ignored or playfully redirected. When necessary, penalties such as "time-out" can be imposed. Penalties will work best, however, if performed promptly. Too often adults allow a child several chances to reform before taking action.

In areas where compliance is not as serious, we can avoid power struggles best by *not* insisting upon immediate satisfaction of our wishes. When we set up a situation so that it's "him or me," our options for walking away from a power struggle become drastically limited. Instead, we can use the broken record technique, try challenging a child to perform the expected behavior, accept (and reinforce) small steps in the direction of the expected behavior, or engage in good old-fashioned bargaining.

The years between two and five are good ones in which to experiment with alternative discipline strategies and identify what works well for both us and the child. We can afford to make mistakes or be downright ineffective without fear that some catastrophe looms on the horizon.

SIX TO ELEVEN—THE LOGICAL AND RIGID SELF

With the onset of the middle years of childhood, cognitive development takes precedence over physical development. As language skills continue to develop, thoughts and verbalizations become more complex and abstract. A child's thinking becomes more logical and his ideas and feelings are communicated more effectively. By drawing on his own past experiences to help him understand present situations, the child begins to see situations from different perspectives. Your son knows, for example, how Mommy must feel when he comes in late for dinner because he can remember how he felt when a friend came late to his party.

Despite this impressive beginning in logical thinking, children have not matured enough at this stage to see the complexities, contradictions, and irrationality in situations. Children see the world as black and white; adults interpret this vision as a kind of rigidity. Children are sure they know what is fair, how things work, and how parents should behave. Members of this age group are particularly susceptible to the influence of television and tend to believe all they hear and see. No amount of discussion can change their minds as their perception of the world is clung to tenaciously.

This seemingly rational being can be very frustrating and demanding. The way a parent dresses may be embarrassing because other parents dress differently. Discipline practices are challenged as unfair. Bedtimes are argued logically. Trying to help such a child see that dress can vary or that discipline decisions are based on a myriad of rational and emotional factors is difficult because the child cannot understand the relevance of these circumstances.

Simultaneously, children this age experience new demands from the outside world. School, peers, and clubs all become part of their day-to-day activities. Their intellectual abilities help them to handle school demands, and the ability to see things from different perspectives facilitates the development of friendships and attachments outside the home. More people become important to the child and more ways of behaving are presented for evaluation. The result of these experiences is that the child's behavior and attitudes are now being influenced by many sources.

Greater exposure to both people and activities heightens a child's ability to evaluate and select. It also causes stress because the child faces demands not only from parents, but also from teachers and friends as well. Succeeding in school (academic), making friends (social), and being involved with religious groups (ethical) are all demanding.

Because children's budding cognitive powers are still limited, adults can not expect to reason everything out. We must take strong, prompt action when children misbehave and we must stand our ground when children try to change our decision. At the same time, adults should show respect for a child's thought powers. Reasons for demands ought to be communicated and discussed at every opportunity. We should also acknowledge the validity of children's arguments and, through gentle questioning, clarify the ambiguity of their viewpoints.

Finally, when a child's thinking is really faulty, it is imperative not to tear it down with glee. You can explain to a child that to you, what the child is saying doesn't make sense and then explain where you think the logic breaks down. The child's thinking can also be dismissed kindly by stating, "Well, we don't see eye-to-eye on this."

It is additionally necessary to let a child know that our authority is not handed down from on high. As children get older and their dealings with the world widen, the basis of adult authority must begin to shift from *telling* to *selling.* Formerly, our authority rested almost entirely on our power to tell children what we wanted and to limit them by our control of nearly all the sources of gratification upon which they are dependent (food, adult attention, toys, etc.). Now, we need to discuss our rules and expectations more and sell them as valuable guidelines for a child's actions. Furthermore, children's reactions to impending decisions which affect their lives ought to be sought. The more children's agreement to decisions can be obtained, the less our authority has to be based on sheer power. If we fail to consult children about matters vital to them, our decisions will need greater enforcement. Making sure that children of this age do what we expect of them, however, is more difficult than it used to be because of their access to a larger social world and the strength of peer influences which may counter adult direction.

The consistency of adult guidance and discipline becomes even more important now because the child is able to evaluate and internalize our standards. Inconsistencies between what we do and what we say will be challenged, and demands for just and fair treatment will be frequent. Even so, adults do not have to become Solomons. Adult fallibility actually helps children by presenting them with the imperfect and sometimes irrational side of life. This enables children to become less rigid in their views and more empathetic toward others,

Children at this age have a special distaste for random exercises of adult authority. They prefer a written list of rules and a schedule of chores to spontaneously delivered commands. They also resent a lot of verbal harassment from adults when responsibilities are forgotten or possessions are lost. Appropriate penalties get a better reception because they appeal to a child's sense of justice and fair play. Some children even suggest a different penalty from the one adults usually impose if the adult's choice has been ineffective. Charting is also appealing as a disciplinary measure.

Finally, we especially need to be careful not to take children's positive actions for granted now that they are older. They still need to be rewarded for their accomplishments and good deeds and need to be given attractive incentives for expectations that have been difficult. Moreover, children may feel overwhelmed at what they must learn and accomplish every day. Consequently, we can help them by monitoring the number of demands we place on them. Succeeding at home, at school, at the playground, and in extracurricular activities may be too much, too soon, and too fast. We often misjudge the amount of demands that six- to eleven-year-old children can handle. They are, after all, still children.

TWELVE TO FIFTEEN—THE QUESTIONING SELF

Parents and teachers get a big surprise as children enter this stage. Even youngsters who were considerate, accepting, and obedient children may suddenly become surly, defensive, and defiant. To make matters worse, a whole list of rules and expectations which had been negotiated and accepted during the previous stage of development are now questioned. Not only do early adolescents expect more and better reasons for our demands, but they also want to know why it is that they cannot be trusted to make all decisions for themselves. What is happening to our children?

One answer, of course, is that with the onset of puberty, extensive physical changes occur which unsettle children. They lose touch with their own identity as if they were immigrants encountering a new country. The rate of these changes is quite variable; some children grow faster or reach sexual maturity sooner than others. Regardless of the rate of development, however, every early adolescent anxiously wonders, "Am I normal?" Adolescents yearn to be normal (which can mean something different for each individual) and inwardly fear they are not; they lose some of the individuality that marked their earlier years. No longer trusting themselves as much, they also distrust adult authority and show it by completely rejecting us at times.

The fundamental insecurity of early adolescents is reflected in their resistance to adult authority, and in their overwhelming need to gain peer acceptance and comfort. Whatever the group is doing is what the individual teen-ager feels he or she should do. And whatever ideas, feelings, and experiences a young teen-ager has must be reported and checked out in detail with friends. The peer group gives the conforming adolescent security, belonging, and a new sense of identity. But peers can also be cruel to and intolerant of those who do not conform.

Cognitively speaking, teen-agers indeed have minds of their own. They are now capable of testing their own actions and the actions of others against ethical values and practical criteria. They can point out the hole in someone's argument and expound upon the implications of another's remarks. They can also see various alternatives in a situation and appreciate the consequences of several courses of action. Unfortunately, they are unlikely to use these intellectual powers for purposes of which adults approve. Rather than be critical of stifling peer group norms or behave like budding scholars in school, young teen-agers much prefer to be critical of their parents' and teachers' directives.

Given these obstacles, there is no question that our authority role must undergo a dramatic shift if we hope young teen-agers will accept any of our previous guidance. As adolescents demand more unilateral decision making, they should be allowed that right. To learn to function independently and to ready themselves to leave home, young teen-agers must begin to accept responsibility for directing their own lives. Paradoxically, the more confidence and trust adults demonstrate to adolescents, the more responsibly young teen-agers will behave. Overprotectiveness, on the other hand, can be perceived as distrust and may foster irresponsible rebellion instead.

This transfer of power needs to be accomplished gradually and steadily. Many adults prefer to hold out as long as possible, hoping that their children won't rebel if given only a little power. It makes more sense to reduce our control over teen-agers by about 10 percent a year (at that rate, they would have near total freedom in their early twenties). To do this wisely, we need to continually examine our priorities and determine which expectations we wish to keep and which we can give up. At first, young teen-agers can be permitted to make relatively insignificant decisions such as having complete choice about whether and what they eat for breakfast. But where they go, when they come home, and how they attend to their household and school responsibilities can still be clearly specified. Year by year, the area of their decision making can increase by whatever degree our best judgment and willingness to take risks dictates.

Of course, we can not always be sure that teen-agers, when left on their own, will make wise choices. We can err by risking too much freedom, but we can also err by failing to trust their capacity to take responsible direction for themselves.

As we slowly phase out our control over children's lives, we can still help teen-agers considerably by being consistently honest about what we think and feel. Directness, even bluntness, is important to model at this time so that teen-agers have a positive example of how to assert themselves with other people. For example, if we disapprove of the behavior of our child's friends, we need to say, "I don't like how your friends act" and then add as many specifics as possible so that what we disapprove of is described clearly. Good eye contact is especially important in these moments of personal disclosure. At the same time, we need to be careful to avoid intimidation or inducement of guilt as we tell teen-agers what's on our minds, and so it's important that our manner is straightforward and nonmanipulative.

Many adults take just the opposite stance. Knowing that teen-agers are suspicious of adult views, they think the best policy is to keep quiet and leave their children or students alone. They are right about the difficulties involved in stating opinions to teen-agers, but they make a big mistake in refraining. Teen-agers still want to know our thoughts and feelings even if they sulk when we share them.

When we do have discussions with young teen-agers, it is helpful to show a genuine interest in what they have to say. Checking out that we are receiving their thinking accurately, acknowledging the validity of their positions, and empathizing with their feelings all help to gain their trust and give them the feeling that communication with us is worthwhile.

In the final analysis, how well we communicate with and influence young teen-agers depends on our ability to *not* take their brashness, criticism, and insensitivity personally. Instead, we can comfort ourselves with the knowledge that from a developmental point of view, their behavior is right on schedule, and should abate if we let go enough to let it happen. Then perhaps they will realize that adults are not so boorish as they once thought. As Mark Twain quipped, "When I was a boy of fourteen, my father was so ignorant I could hardly stand to have the old man around, but when I got to be twenty-one, I was astonished at how much he had learned in seven years."

FIFTEEN TO TWENTY—THE INDEPENDENT SELF

After the initial adjustment to adolescence, there emerges an individual in search of autonomy, personal independence, and the courage to exercise adult rights. The goal of this stage of development is to become prepared financially, psychologically, intellectually, and ethically to leave home and live in the world as a self-reliant adult. The years of adult guidance, training, and protection are coming to an end. Now home, school, and peers all become a laboratory in which the adolescent tests his readiness for independence.

Older adolescents need to try their wings in a variety of ways. Intimate relationships outside the home enable teen-agers to feel confident that they can have close relationships with others outside their family. Experimenting with sex, alcoholic drinking, and drugs helps them learn how much they can trust themselves. Part-time jobs give a sense of security that someday soon they will have the means to live independently. Making decisions about religious observance tests the parental values young adults need to either accept or revise. Contemplating plans about career, lifestyle, and education help to clarify future directions.

This agenda of activity sounds so reasonable but rarely proceeds smoothly. When adolescents do let themselves try out their wings, they often flop. They come home drunk; they get involved in hair-brained money-making schemes; they decide to quit school in order to work; or they don't find a job because they don't have the qualifications. Their own pipe dreams go up in smoke.

But there's another side to this story. Both parents and teachers, with the best of intentions, inadvertently sabotage the adolescent's independence training by giving inconsistent messages. They want their teen-agers to *act* like adults but not to *become* adults. Parents and teachers have difficulty letting go and allowing adolescents the freedom to make their own decisions, and consequently create roadblocks that even the most level-headed adolescent could not surmount.

Because parents and teachers know how hard it is to be successful adults, they load up adolescents with advice, some appropriate and some inappropriate. Sometimes however, by insisting that adolescents accept their advice, they initiate a premature departure. Adolescents need to determine whether our wisdom is applicable for them. With support, they will often behave very rationally and develop plans that are realistic. Just one caveat: The plans will be their plans, not ours; their dreams, not ours. In the best situations, their plans will coincide with our hopes for them. But we must also be prepared for a teen-ager's completely different set of decisions.

Because the task of this age group is to leave home, conflict is inevitable. The amount of conflict, however, depends to a great extent upon adult expectations of adolescents. Many people expect these years to be a time of crisis, stress, rebellion, wild abandon, and general irresponsibility. Those who act according to these expectations are likely to get them fulfilled. While stress is inevitable at this stage, we need to be mindful that the degree of stress and conflict depends, in large measure, on parental and societal reactions to adolescents.

The societal phenomenon of prolonged adolescence deserves mention here. Because technological advances require increasingly more education and training, some adolescents, in order to reach career goals, feel forced to continue accepting financial support from their parents for much longer than they would like. This tie to home retards an adolescent's sense of independence and self-sufficiency. While there is nothing inherently good or bad about financial support, reactions of the involved parties can create conflict. Should financial support be interpreted by the parent as carrying with it the right to intrude on other areas of the adolescent's life, the adolescent will feel burdened and resent the assistance. Establishing the amount of support, its time span and purpose—in general, being clear about the support—is the key to minimizing conflict and to strengthening the relationship.

Finally, it should be stressed that some rules of conduct for adolescents in our homes are still appropriate. We don't need to accommodate the family's life-style to the wishes of an adolescent. In fact, making life too easy at home may inhibit the adolescent's drive for independence. For example, if parents are available for total financial support, the teen-ager may have less desire to get a job. If adults are available for primary relationships, the adolescent may feel less need to seek companionship from peers. Letting an adolescent know that we care and wish them well is important. If an experiment flops, we'll be there for support but not to pick up the pieces. The adolescent is in training for independence and that means learning to be responsible for flops. As the trainee's manager, we must allow the adolescent to learn from the natural consequences of his actions. Whether an adolescent permanently leaves home after a bloody battle or after a hug is, in part, up to us.

8 | The Balance Between Involvement and Detachment

A mother writes: "I took my youngest child to the dentist for her first installment in the seige of braces. It was to be a fifteen-minute appointment and they wanted to see her alone. She came out of the room crying and sped right to our car. I got into the back seat with her and asked her what happened. She said she wanted to go home. We did.

"She ran straight to her room and I asked her if I could stay. She shrugged her shoulders. I decided to interpret the shrug as yes and I sat next to her and let her cry. She cried, but with her back to me, not letting me in. I did not talk to her because in the past this has made things worse. After what seemed like a long time, I asked her if she could tell me what had happened. She said she couldn't, so I told her I was going to leave her for a while.

"When I came back I said, 'Katey, would you like me to give you a backrub?'
'No'.
'Katey, would you like me to give you a foot massage?'
'No'.
'Would you like me to hold you?'
'No'.
'Would you like me to give you five elephants?' Her body moved.
'Katey, would you like me to give you four speckled puppies?'

A noise. I kept on asking about giving her more and more outrageous things and pretty soon she was laughing.

"She put a pillow over her face and I tried to take it away. I was at first afraid it would make her mad and it did. She began to kick me. I realized that she couldn't be depressed if she were mad. I began to creepy-mouse my fingers up to the pillow and try to snatch it away. She kept hitting out at me. Then I put my arms around her and held on. She began to fight. It became a roughhouse—on to the floor, back on the bed. I tried to be careful to let her be stronger than me. All of this time she tried to cover her head with a pillow or blanket. There was a lot of laughter from her now.

"Then I began to drag her about pretending to be a monster and making monster noises. After the monster, I pretended to give her a shot in her arm, then in each toe, then in her hip. She fought each one laughing. By then I was exhausted and had to go down and start supper.

"After supper was underway she came downstairs with the hood of her sweater over her face and began to dance around me. I was on the telephone and once or twice she came at me and quickly raised and lowered the hood showing me her teeth. I realized that something important was happening. When I finished on the telephone, I followed her upstairs and caught her in the bathroom. She sat down on the seat and pulled a nearby towel over her face. I began to talk to her in a high creaky voice and said things such as: 'Open wide. This won't hurt at all. This won't take long.' All the things that doctors say to you. Lots of laughter. Then she took a small piece of toilet paper and put it in her mouth, between her lips as if it were a tooth. She pulled it out and gave it to me. I told her she was naughty (a word I never use) and not to pull her teeth out like that but to put them back because I had to do something to her teeth. Then she put more 'teeth' in her mouth and began to spit them at me. Laughter. 'Open wide, this won't hurt,' and so on.

"Then I went downstairs to check on supper and up again to ask her to come down to eat it. She began then to really cry. She took me from her room into the bathroom where there is a mirror and showed me the bands they had put on her teeth. She said they hurt her. She didn't know if she could eat, but she would try some on a tray. She ate it all and then came downstairs. She was perky and talked on and on about her dentist experience.

I never felt so wonderful about anything I have done."

Here is a parent trying to achieve a delicate balance between intruding on her daughter and staying away. We have shown this letter to many people. Some like the balance achieved by the mother; some dislike it. Which opinion should reign is immaterial because the balance each of us seeks with our children has to fit our personality and the child's needs.

Without question, we can enjoy a more assertive relationship with children if we learn how to talk and present ourselves effectively, to avoid power struggles, and to adjust to the changes in child development. Improvement in even one of these areas can increase our confidence as adult authority figures. But growth in assertiveness can be shortlived if unhealthy patterns of emotional involvement with children interfere. Children will not ultimately accept our authority when they sense that our expectations satisfy personal needs more than they provide reasonable direction for them. Nor will children entrust us with a measurable degree of control over their lives if they sense that we will not give them attention and care. When we are emotionally entangled or withdrawn in our relationship with children, chances are that assertive skills, creative discipline methods, and knowledge of child development will not bale us out.

The importance of emotional involvement can also be stated positively. When our relationship with children reflects a healthy balance between involvement and detachment, it is much easier to talk and act assertively, to avoid power struggles, and to adjust our authority role as children grow. This pleasant state of affairs happens because the right blend of involvement and detachment enables us to feel less guilty about our intentions as parents and teachers.

Much of the credit for insisting that healthy adult involvement and effective discipline are inseparable goes to William Glasser. Glasser maintains that *being involved* with children, that is, being warm, personal, and interested in them, is an absolutely necessary first step in helping children become more responsible to themselves and to others. Without an adult's caring, he argues, children will resist an adult's guidance and direction. Moreover, children learn how to make better and more responsible choices about their behavior by identifying with their parents and teachers. This identification, in Glasser's view, does not take place unless children feel that adults are involved with them.

Another major contention by Glasser is that adult caring helps children to develop a positive feeling of self-worth. Children assume that they must be worthwhile if adults take the trouble to involve themselves in the children's lives. This sense of self-worth is critical because, according to Glasser, "people act in accordance with how they see themselves." If children view themselves positively, they will behave positively.

In our workshops for parents and teachers, we have found that most participants readily accept Glasser's wisdom. But we have also found that they have some pointed concerns. They want to know concretely what is too much involvement and what is too little. They want to understand the quality of their current involvement with children. They want to know why it is that their own children seem to resist adult involvement. Finally, they want to feel encouraged that an unsatisfactory, yet long-standing pattern of involvement with their children can be reversed. Our answers to these questions will be shared with you here.

THE ROAD TO INVOLVEMENT WITH CHILDREN

Getting involved with children is one of the most taxing and challenging of human tasks. In today's society, we can rightly be impressed by the desire to even have children. In the past, children were an economic necessity, helping a family to divide labor and generate income. Now they have become an economic burden, costing us thousands of dollars yearly for food, clothing, education, and the many other goods and services we must purchase. We are warned that children are not our domain or property. As Kahlil Gibran proclaims in *The Prophet,* "Your children are not your children. They are the sons and daughters of Life's longing for itself. They come through you but not from you. And though they are with you yet they belong not to you." For both parents and teachers, a child's journey leads to eventual separation and emptiness. Still, many adults are willing to care for children anyway. Why?

Consider why you have chosen to be a parent or teacher. Try to recall the circumstances leading up to this decision and the thoughts and feelings which attended it. Do you remember how freely you discussed the matter with your spouse, your parents, friends, relatives and coworkers? Was it an active decision that you made or one that just happened? Were you fearful? Relieved? Indifferent? Confident? What else? Stop and think about these questions for a moment.

In preparing this book, we asked several adults the question, "What influenced you to be a parent or teacher?" As you might expect, this question revealed a wide variety of needs and motives. Some respondents emphasized what they *would give to children.* Some who were interviewed stressed what children *would give to them.* Still others had no intentions of their own; they were content or compelled to satisfy the expectations of others.

Here is a sample of what they said:

- "I had little choice but to become a teacher."
- "I felt that having a child was what I was supposed to do."
- "Children would bring happiness and meaning to my life."
- "I had a tradition I wanted to pass down."
- "I wanted to give children what I didn't get as a child."
- "Everyone else I knew was having children."
- "I felt I could do better than the teachers I had as a student."
- "I wanted some small sense of immortality."
- "Children would teach me things about life that I have forgotten or ignored."
- "I really enjoy children."
- "It was time to settle down and have a family."
- "I wanted to prove to myself that I could have children."
- "I hoped it would help my marriage."

When we probed farther, we discovered that the actual entrance into parenthood or the classroom affected people in different ways. For some, the feelings and attitudes that attended their decision to parent or teach played a minor role in their developing relationship with children. For others, the role was a major one. Following are some dramatic examples:

1. Bill felt left out of the decision to become a parent. His wife intentionally stopped using contraceptives without his knowledge, and became pregnant. Because he could not deal with his anger and the insult of being excluded, he feigned cooperation and pleasantness during the pregnancy. When the child arrived, however, he avenged his wife by being excessively critical of her behavior as a mother, yet remained aloof from the child.

2. Martha worked very hard at her career in psychiatric social work. Late hours, emergency calls, continual crises at the agency for which she worked had taken their toll. She decided it would be much easier and more rewarding to take care of her own child than to tolerate the problem people at the agency. Being a mother, however, turned out to be a disillusioning experience. It was often even more frustrating than psychiatric social work; when it wasn't frustrating, it was boring and unrewarding. Arranging as much child care as she could, Martha seized the first opportunity she could to return to her career.

3. Rachel always thought she was effective with children. When she was a teen-ager, children seemed to like her and she always felt more comfortable with them than with adults. Moreover, from her student teaching experience she was convinced that she could be more creative and open with children than any of her teachers had been with her. Sure enough, once in charge of her own classroom, a warm relationship between Rachel and most of her students quickly blossomed. Given the freedom to explore and create, the children also found learning to be fun. But a few children rejected her approach and were sullen and unproductive. Taking this as a sign of failure, Rachel poured all her energy into winning over these students. The more she hovered over them, reaching for their warmth and responsiveness, the more they rejected her efforts. It wasn't long before teacher and students became enmeshed in endless conflict over the value of learning and acceptance of Rachel as the teacher.

4. Brenda and Dave got married in their early twenties and vowed to each other not to have children until they were really "to-gether" as a couple. For five years, they had considerable tension and despair together. Desperate to shore up the relationship between them, they decided to have a child despite their previous vow. As the child grew up, she was showered with love, attention, and protection. They would never entrust her to a baby-sitter when she was an infant. They read poetry to her daily when she was three. Throughout her early childhood, she was taken to every activity or source of entertainment known to exist for children.

Most of us are not so different from the people who were interviewed. Positive and negative factors probably influenced our willingness to take on the obligation of children. And possibly, once we actually came into close contact with children, patterns of involvement developed which were not totally healthy. Although that possibility does not make us unstable and immature, we should realize that *adults rarely form ideal relationships with children.* In different degrees, we all have emotional limitations. There is hardly a person alive who doesn't have some unfulfilled desire to feel needed, loved, or strong. Sometimes we may hope that children represent an opportunity to get those needs met. Through them, we can feel adequate and complete, and so we expect them to live for us. Yet at other times, we may believe that children represent a hindrance in our lives. If it weren't for them, we could really be successful and happy. So we expect them to leave us alone.

We can think of our resulting relationships with children as falling along a continuum of emotional involvement. At one extreme of the continuum is a relationship marked by *disengagement.* At the other end is a relationship marked by *overinvolvement.*

A disengaged relationship is one in which an adult is emotionally distant from a child or group of children. The adult's goal (sometimes conscious, sometimes not) is to *avoid* children in order to achieve personal needs. An overinvolved relationship is one in which an adult is emotionally entangled with a child or group of children. The adult's goal is to *use* children to achieve personal needs.

The concepts of disengagement and overinvolvment may seem quite simple on the surface, but in reality are quite complex. For example:

- People are neither totally disengaged nor totally overinvolved with children. It is more accurate to say that they tend to be more overinvolved than disengaged or vice versa.
- Relationships can fluctuate. Although some adults consistently maintain a pattern of disengagement or overinvolvement with children, many move back and forth along the continuum, even with the same child.
- It is quite common for an adult to be overinvolved with one child in a family or classroom while disengaged with other children.
- Adults are not necessarily overinvolved or disengaged in *every* area of their relationships with children. A teacher may be physically distant from her children but overin-

volved socially. Or a parent may be overinvolved with his teen-ager's school performance but avoids any encounter with the teen-ager's attitudes toward sex.

• The psychological traits of parents or teachers do not, by themselves, determine their tendency toward overinvolvement or disengagement. Usually, the level of involvement of any adult is influenced by the roles assumed by others in the family or the school community. In a family system, it is common to find a mother and father assuming opposite levels of emotional involvement with all or some of their children. In a school, a teacher may become disengaged or overinvolved in response to the attitudes and behaviors of colleagues, parents, or administrators.

• Nonassertive and aggressive behavior can occur both in disengaged and overinvolved relationships. An adult can be distant and harsh or distant and permissive. Or an adult can be overinvolved and harsh or overinvolved and permissive.

Before a more detailed description of disengagement and overinvolvement is given, take a moment and think about your experience as a parent or teacher. When you consider the questions below, reflect on your overall relationship to children as well as your relationship with specific children in your family or classroom.

1. To what extent do you feel comfortable being with your children/students? Do you often feel like being somewhere else?

2. How close do you need your children/students to be to you? Are you able to tolerate emotional distance and lack of communication from your children/students?

3. How enthusiastic are you about being a parent or teacher? Were you once excited about it but now feel disillusioned or indifferent?

4. How important is it that your children's/students' behavior and accomplishments reflect well on you? Do you worry a lot that your children's/students' misbehavior or lack of skill will embarrass you?

5. How active a role do you take in your parenting or teaching? Do your spouse or colleagues get more involved with children than you do?

6. How much do you keep after your children/students about their behavior? Are you usually dissatisfied about what they do and show your dissatisfaction in a resentful way?

DISENGAGEMENT

When adults are disengaged from children, the message they send is "leave me alone." Rarely is this message actually stated nor is it often meant so bluntly. For most adults, it is more a subtle plea than an order. By limiting communication to the minimum necessary for transacting family or classroom business, disengaged adults let children know that they don't want to get too involved with them.

Disengaged adults are often silent at the dinner table or in the family car or before class is called to order. They frequently tune out when children talk to them and look for escape routes when children pressure them. Such adults are less likely to *initiate* words of guidance, support, or encouragement. When something happens that displeases them, they may speak up, even explode, but then often return to silence.

Disengaged adults can be quite firm and demanding. If they are, however, their authority style is rather rigid. Rules and expectations are rarely reviewed to determine if they require revision. Reasons are seldom given for authoritative action. Children are simply told what adults want. These adults can also be weak and permissive. Such traits are frequently accompanied by a friendliness and warmth which are genuine as long as children do not demand too much attention. If they do, these adults get cranky.

Feelings of disillusionment characterize many disengaged parents and teachers. Parents may hope that children will bring them a respite from their careers. Or they may expect children to give them a feeling of self-worth or a stronger connection to their spouse. When these hopes are dashed, the emotional bond with children is severed and replaced by indifference, disappointment, or even rage. Teachers are similarly disillusioned. Some hope that children come to them to learn but discover that their job amounts largely to custodial care. Or some expect to work closely with and get support from other adults, both parents and professional colleagues, but instead, find that parents blame them a lot and other teachers are competitive or simply keep to themselves. As a result, they lose involvement in their work and consequently in their students.

There is also a tendency when adults are disengaged to be rather complacent about what is happening in the life struggles of children. When a child is going through a rough period of development, the disengaged adult is eager to adopt the attitude that "this too shall pass," or "it's just a phase." When a child's behavior is really disturbing, there is a great deal of wishful thinking but little action, on the part of the disengaged adult. Above all else, disengaged adults tend to dislike intervening in children's lives. It is not uncommon to find attitudes such as: "My children (students) can do no wrong"; "They can do no better"; "I'll be there if they really need me"; or "I'd rather leave them alone."

Why do so many adults disengage from children in the ways we've described? The reasons are varied.

A small minority of adults are actually uninterested in children. W. C. Field's wisecrack, "I like children, yes I do; baked or fried in a stew" is a fair (albeit exaggerated) representation of their feelings. Often raised by cold, aloof, perhaps even physically abusive parents, they simply failed to receive the emotional nourishment which could be given, in turn, to their children or students. If confronted with their uninterest in children, they may reply, "That's just the way I am. I wasn't meant to have kids," or "Our family was always unemotional."

A large number of parents and teachers are forced into a position of disengagement by economic and personal demands made on their lives. Public figures and adults who must hold down several jobs to provide for their family are often a part of this group. Also included are people whose energies are severely drained by the needs of other adults dependent on them and those who lack any substantial emotional support for themselves. In some cases, adults use these predicaments as an excuse for disengagement and fail to plan for quality time with children. In other cases, adults are honestly overwhelmed and often run out of time and energy.

An even larger number of disengaged adults are people like Willy Loman, the legendary character in Arthur Miller's *Death of a Salesman*. They are interested in supporting and guiding children but, excessively preoccupied with their own conflicts and worries, are too emotionally blocked to do it. In an effort to control their own lives, they build walls around themselves to get distance not only from children but other adults as well. They swing in mood from heightened self-doubt to wide-eyed optimism. Needing to rationalize their own failures, they are quick to rationalize away the importance of problems faced by their children or students. Finding so much fault with themselves, they are reluctant to find anything wrong with children.

Yet as we have said, disengagement is not solely determined by emotional blocks. It is also a result of what is happening within a family or school system. A disengaged adult is often found, for example, in a family system in which his or her spouse is overly involved with the children. The disengaged parent serves, then, as a balance to the overinvolved parent. Sometimes this is a position that the disengaged parent readily favors (since he or she is then allowed to remain withdrawn from the parent-child battleground). Frequently, though, the disengaged parent wants to intervene with the children (especially if he or she disapproves of the parenting style of the other parent) but is blocked access by the overinvolved parent and even by the children.* As a result, the disengaged parent feels trapped and unable to change.

In a school system, disengaged teachers are products of being placed in impossible situations by school administrators and parents. For example, their major responsibilities as teachers may be poorly defined. One day they are expected to stress academics, but the next day they are asked to emphasize values. They may also be tossed from pillar to post on contrasting expectations such as fostering creative thinking as opposed to promoting the learning of facts; planning lessons with behavioral objectives as opposed to being spontaneous and open-ended; insisting that standards are maintained as opposed to avoiding failure and nonpromotion. The amount of freedom or leeway teachers have to use their own professional judgment to cope with these contrasting expectations is also unclear. The result is a kind of paralysis; teachers are too confused to be engaged with their students. And because teachers

---

*Such a dynamic is difficult to recognize when the overinvolved parent ostensibly invites the disengaged parent to intervene with the children. ("I have to be the mean one in the family. Why can't you be the 'heavy' once in a while?") Usually such invitations are setups to prove the incompetence of the disengaged parent and thereby allow the overinvolved parent to maintain his or her position in the family system.

are so professionally isolated from each other, they feel helpless to change their situation.

In light of all the negative reasons for adult disengagement, one could assume that its effects are always negative. However, there is a positive side to adult disengagement because children are not constantly harassed or made to feel that their parents' or teacher's self-esteem rides on everything they do. But adult disengagement can also have two dangerous effects on children: (1) Children can be seduced into believing that they have more—and should continue to maintain more—emotional independence from adults than is really healthy for them, and (2) children are denied the security that they can depend on active adult support.

OVERINVOLVEMENT

When adults are overinvolved with children, the message they send is, "I live through you." They expect a closeness between them and children which the latter find overwhelming and often suffocating.

Overinvolvement is sometimes difficult to recognize because on the surface it can look like healthy caring. This misperception occurs because overinvolved adults often have considerable love and concern for children and spend a generous amount of time with them. They also tend to be convinced that all the time and energy given to their children is vitally necessary. Some of the negative reasons for their involvement in children are thereby camouflaged.

Overinvolved adults intrude into children's lives. This intrusion is also difficult to recognize because it appears in different guises. Some adults intrude, for example, by inappropriately seeking their children's friendship. A child may even have been told he is one of the adult's best friends. Because the adult is turning to a child for love and counsel, it becomes unclear who is performing the role of child and who the role of adult. One of the ways this love and counsel is sought is in expressing personal feelings of weakness, sadness, or frustration to a child, hoping the child, in turn, will be soothing and comforting. Another tactic is expressing a need to be a child's confidant, hoping to gain the opportunity to unburden oneself in exchange.

Using children inappropriately for emotional support frequently occurs because adults fail to develop adequate relationships with other adults or to create other dimensions in their lives beyond their involvement with children. Both parents and teachers sometimes feel isolated from stimulating adult contact. Many cope with this fact by making projects of their children or students. Instead of seeking peer stimulation, whether personal or professional, they seize every opportunity to become immersed in their children. As a result, their successes and failures with children are invested with an inordinate degree of importance. Everything the children do is allowed to reflect on them.*

A closely related form of intrusion occurs when adults have far too many expectations of and preferences for children. They care about *all* the foods they eat, *all* the clothes they wear, and *all* the details of how homework is to be done. They tend to have overly high standards ("You only got a B?") and are overactive in praising and criticizing children's behavior. Typically, such adults insist that their children keep them steadily and completely informed of their thoughts, feelings, and experiences, and react immediately to any variation in their children's mood. Interrogations like, "What's the matter?" "Why are you frowning?" "What are you thinking about?" flow without abatement. Moreover, any conflicts between such adults and children are usually pursued until the adult is satisfied with the resolution. Children are not allowed to walk out in the heat of battle and if they do, they are followed. Children are rarely allowed to escape conflict, discomfort, and humiliation.

These overinvolved adults often communicate with children but have difficulty controlling themselves. They may interrupt when children are talking, monopolize and redirect conversation, and simply fail to listen and check out what their children are saying. In conflict situations, they move quickly from debate about the issue at hand to power struggles. It often seems that such parents or teachers are capable of saying anything, from expression of deeply felt love to explosive hatred.

The boundary between the children's area of freedom and responsibility and the adult's domain is blurred in an overinvolved relationship. The parent or teacher frequently takes charge of the problems faced by children and tries to solve them on their behalf.

*Such an intense involvement with children was vividly portrayed, for example, in the play and movie, *The Prime of Miss Jean Brodie*.

A mother who arranges for other children to play with her shy child without prior consultation is such a parent. This overprotection can be extremely harmful when it interferes with a child's access to peer relationships. For example, a school counselor told us about a mother who felt so overprotective of her daughter that she began a pattern of finding fault with all her daughter's friends, even manipulating situations and facts to prove that these were unworthy friends. Although the daughter initially resisted these accusations, over time she became convinced by her mother's misperceptions. By age seventeen, the daughter had no friends, few social skills, and many self-doubts.

The boundary between what has already happened in an over-involved relationship and what is presently happening is blurred, as well. Often, the past failures and transgressions of the child are invoked when the present difficulties are being discussed. Instead of feeling that a fresh start is possible, children are made to feel trapped by their past. They develop an overwhelming sense that they are stereotyped for life, as, for example, an unfriendly child. This stigma is particularly frustrating because overinvolved adults also tend not to give up. Despite their penchant for labeling, they usually exert strong pressure on their children to overcome their shortcomings.

The positive aspects of adult overinvolvement are plain to see. Children are assured that they can turn to their parents or teachers for support whenever it is needed. There is also little ambiguity where overinvolved parents and teachers stand on matters, a sense which can be far more reassuring than the absence of communication of disengaged adults. Children of overinvolved parents or teachers can feel some sense of personal importance. They realize that the adults need them very much.

The cost children pay from adult overinvolvement is the lack of space in which to grow independent of adult direction. Although children surely benefit from the push adults provide to work hard, develop new skills, and seek new experiences, the push of an overinvolved adult is often too forceful. What's worse, the push can sometimes be toward a goal in which the adult is too involved. Imagine the special pressures to stay thin incurred by a child of an obese parent. Think of the burden a child carries from a parent who never quite made it as an athlete, or an English teacher who never quite made it as a writer. Absorbing the unfulfilled hopes and aspirations of adults extracts a big price from children.

Adults often complain that their honest overtures to be interested in their children's problems, to share their own thoughts and feelings, and simply to have some fun time with their children are almost universally rejected. It is true that some of that rejection can be dismissed (however painful that may be) as children's desire to be separate from adult authority and control. However, a lot of that rejection stems from adult overinvolvement. Children recognize that their own search for identity is being seriously compromised by their parents' or teachers' desire to satisfy personal needs through them.

THE IMPACT OF OVERINVOLVEMENT AND DISENGAGEMENT ON ADULT AUTHORITY

When we are disengaged or overinvolved, our ability to maintain an assertive authority role is seriously jeopardized. The reasons are different, however, for each end of the continuum.

To a child's mind, the realm of authority and the realm of relationship are intertwined. Children don't necessarily accept the word of authority because it is just or wise. Until adolescence, their conceptions of justice and the social order may not be sufficiently developed to respect a rule solely on its merits. To really accept authority imposed on them, it is necessary for children (more than for adults) to feel a solid personal connection with the person directing that authority. In some respects, it's a trade-off. Often, children willingly comply (even though they may be unconvinced of the *wisdom* of adult demands or refusals) if they, in exchange, can have a close and caring relationship with adults. They don't have that quality of relationship with disengaged adults. As a result, when disengaged adults try to assert authority, children tend to perceive it as arbitrary, unfair, or mean, even when it is none of these things. Children sulk, drag their heels, and use other passive-aggressive strategies to avoid compliance.

Another major problem for some disengaged authority figures is that they receive little information about their children's actions. Children are usually more wary of disengaged adults than overinvolved adults. As we have mentioned, the former are less likely to take a persistent, active role in disciplining children and are more likely to react adversely or arbitrarily when something bothers them at any given moment. Consequently, children can't easily predict when they might get into trouble. To defend themselves, they frequently lie or conceal any behavior which might be frowned upon. This secrecy is sometimes abetted by another parent or teacher who protects the child by urging, "You better not let your father/mother/teacher know about this."

While children try to sidetrack the authority of disengaged adults, they usually engage in active power struggles with overinvolved adults. Sensing the overinvolved adult's vulnerability to losing a child's love or approval, resourceful children can easily manipulate them into a tug of war of intimidation and guilt. They might fly into fits of rage, cry uncontrollably, pout, talk back, or use other power tactics to get adults to back down. If adults are threatened by these actions, they typically respond in kind. The battle then continues until the child is placated, the adult wins a fleeting victory, or a stalemate occurs which leaves both parties miserable. To put it simply, a child has a lot of leverage in an overinvolved relationship.

Of course, it is precisely because *control* is such a vital issue in the relationship between overinvolved adults and children that these power struggles occur. The adults make demands of their children on many fronts at once (all the way from emotional solace to what children do during their spare time), so the children feel unable to please them. Children resent their predicament and assume that the only way they can change it is to control the adults by resisting almost everything the adults demand of them.

The kind of involvement with our children that enhances assertive authority avoids the pitfalls of extreme disengagement or overinvolvement. We are willing to relate to children with caring, support, and an openness to mutual sharing. At the same time, there is some distance and separation so that we do not have to control each other to have our needs met. Children are given space to grow, but are not denied guidance and counsel. Above all else, we act as parents and teachers; we do not become benevolent dictators who assume infinite wisdom and control, nor do we pretend that we are merely friends, without special responsibilities.

BREAKING PATTERNS OF DISENGAGEMENT AND OVERINVOLVEMENT

It is possible for the most silent, withdrawn parents to become actively involved with their children. We have seen it happen a number of times. We have also witnessed remarkable changes in the involvement level of previously dispirited, disengaged teachers. It is just as possible for parents and teachers who allow their own egos to be on the line every time a child succeeds or fails to learn to emotionally detach themselves. Although the breaking of severe patterns of disengagement and overinvolvement requires professional counseling or psychotherapy, the everyday variety can be altered considerably with some remedies that can be used at home or in the classroom. What follows are suggestions and activities to help you move toward greater involvement or separation from the children in your charge. Choose those that apply best to you and give them a concerted try.

Seeking Help For Yourself

The false idea that people can change by themselves was discussed in chapter 1. Seeking help is not a sign of weakness but of personal strength. If you don't seek the help of others close to you, they will more than likely interfere with your efforts to change. The "old you" is predictable, and will be preferred unless you encourage others to accept a "new you."

If you feel disengaged from your children, talk over the problem with your spouse. Tell him or her, "I want to be more included with the children. What can we do to make it possible for me to have a strong role with them? What do we do that blocks that from happening now?" If your spouse puts down your request by saying, for example, "How come all of a sudden you want to get involved?" don't argue or defend yourself. Simply reply, "I want to know my children better and I want to guide them more. Can you help me to do this?"

When overinvolvement seems to be more of a problem than disengagement, it is imperative to examine to what extent you have developed a sufficient number of adult friendships and outside interests. Ask yourself: "Do I really share my problems with my spouse or my friends? Am I so wrapped up in my children that I haven't allowed for other outlets in my life? Who can I seek for support and help? What can I be doing that will feel productive and yet give me some healthy distance from my children?"

Professional help is, of course, an important means of support. When parents find themselves disengaged or overinvolved with children, they should consider going to a child guidance clinic, a mental health center, or a private psychologist who practices family therapy. A family therapist works with the entire family (although not necessarily at each session), regardless of how severe the symptoms or problems of any one of its members are. This enables the therapist to facilitate changes which will not get undermined or sabotaged by others in the family. Family therapists also tend to work quickly, thereby avoiding years of professional counseling. Certified family therapists belong to the American Association of Marriage and Family Therapists.

Teachers, as we have noted, become easily disengaged from or overinvolved with their students because of their professional isolation. Teachers need to be brought together! One of the ways this can be done is through *team teaching,* which allows joint responsibility for a group of students, usually with a careful plan for dividing responsibilities and allowing each team member to teach the subjects he or she teaches best. *Professional support groups* is another way. This entails scheduled and informal get-togethers to discuss common concerns and problems, share ideas, and identify ways to help each other. *Peer supervision counseling,* which pairs teachers to observe each other (if possible) and provide feedback, counsel, and a sympathetic ear, can also help.

It is possible for schools to get a kind of organizational therapy by obtaining the services of professionals in the field of organizational development and planned change. These people are often highly successful in bringing about a feeling of renewed energy and direction at a school in which teachers have become disengaged from their work, and consequently from their students.*

---

*A good introductory description of organizational development in schools is found in Richard A. Schmuck and Patricia A. Schmuck, *A Humanistic Psychology of Education: Making the School Everybody's House* (Palo Alto: National Press Books, 1974).

Quality Time with Individual Children

One-to-one, quality contacts with children are very important in building relationships. You learn about a child's interests, concerns, and style, and they learn about yours. A bond grows between you that strengthens the influence you can have with the child without becoming overinvolved.

The important principle in selecting what you do for quality time is to identify *underdeveloped areas of activity between you and the child.* If there has not been enough talk between you, arrange time to talk. If there has not been enough calming silence when you have been together previously, do something which is relatively quiet, such as painting, star-gazing, reading a story, seeing a movie, playing board games, or listening to music. If most everything you do together is sedentary, do something active or physical, like camping, hiking, jogging, wood building, making crafts, flying a kite, modeling, or cycling. Finally, if you tend to always play together, do some constructive work, such as repairing something, baking and cooking, car washing, shopping, gardening, where the child can feel some valuable contribution is being made.*

One-to-one quality time is particularly helpful with a child from whom you have been more disengaged than other children in your family or classroom. A friend shared with us a personal story which illustrates this point. Although he had always been very involved with his oldest son, David, he realized that his relationship with his next son, Benjamin, had been distant. So he decided to buy two carving knives, one for himself and one for Benjamin, and invited Benjamin to learn woodcarving with him. Rather than feel compelled to be a fair father and buy David a carving knife also, the father explained to David his wish to do something special with Benjamin, assuring David that they would remain close in other ways. David accepted his father's action, and Benjamin and his father enjoyed a new chance to develop their relationship.

Private rap time presents some special challenges for adults who have disengaged or overinvolved relationships with children. If you have been fairly noncommunicative with a child, begin

*See Sutton-Smith, B. and Sutton-Smith, S., *How to Play With Your Children (and When Not To)* (New York: Hawthorn Books, Inc., 1974) for other ideas about play and work with children.

finding ways to volunteer information about your thoughts and feelings. Tell the child about yourself—your life experiences, particularly your childhood; your knowledge about a subject that might be of mutual interest; your reactions to people, places, and events you have shared, and even your attitudes toward religion, society, family life, and personal responsibility. As you talk, allow opportunities for the child to respond. Let your conversation flow. It's best if the talk happens without your thinking too much about it.*

If you have been overinvolved with a child, it is crucial that you begin to find ways to reduce your monopoly over conversations. As an experiment, try for one week to *listen to the child more than you talk*. Draw out your child's ideas, experiences, and feelings. Avoid mind reading and instant judgment. Don't decide too quickly what the child is really saying, or evaluate too soon whether or not you like what you are hearing.

Consider conducting a structured interview† with the child if you feel that your attempts at a private time to talk will not go well. You might tell the child that you read in a book a fun idea that you'd like to try. It involves acting like a reporter and asking each other some questions for a personal portrait in a magazine. Here are some questions that can be provided:

- Have you ever been lucky?
- What was the scariest experience you ever had?
- What's your favorite (color, day, season, book, TV program, singing group, food, place to visit)?
- What do you think you'll be doing in ten years?
- Do you remember your dreams?

*Even very young children benefit from your conversation. A fun and moving experience for any parent is to invent stories and stir children's imagination instead of relying on printed books. I created for my children a character who was the strongest person in the world. Unfortunately, no one wanted to have him at their house because, given his enormous strength, he would unintentionally break things. The strong man lived alone in the forest, emerging only to help children in distress. Week after week, my children begged me to spin yarns about this character who was merely a figment of my imagination. Any story would do, so I didn't have to be the world's best storyteller. To this day, we share fond memories of these stories.
†This technique is excellent for elementary school teachers. During the first month of the school year, it should be possible to get around to each student and have this private experience.

- Describe the best teacher you ever had.
- What is the earliest memory you have?
- Have you ever been really sick?
- What do you look for in a friend?
- What is your biggest gripe about our family/class?
- What do you like best about our family/class?
- What's the thing you like best about yourself?
- What's the thing you like least about yourself?

Communicating Positive Expectations

Remember *My Fair Lady*? In addition to its effectiveness as a musical show, it taught a powerful lesson in human relations: How we treat a person communicates our expectations or predictions about how that person will behave in the future. These expectations, in turn, have the effect of self-fulfilling prophecies. People to whom we communicate negative expectations tend to respond negatively; people for whom we have positive expectations tend to respond positively. As Liza Doolittle puts it, "I shall always be a flower girl to Professor Higgins, because he always treats me as a flower girl, and always will; but I know I can be a lady to you, because you always treat me as a lady, and always will."

Both overinvolved and disengaged adults can improve the quality of their relationships with children by being purveyors of positive expectations. Actively communicating positive expectations is an effective antidote for both an attitude of complacency and an attitude of chronic dissatisfaction toward children. You're letting children know, without nagging, that you believe in their potential even if their present behavior doesn't meet your standards.

The key to communicating positive expectations is to identify specific ways you can show children that you believe in them and that you will not give up on their capacity to grow and change. Consider the following suggestions.

For Parents:
1. Give your children some control over when and how they fulfill your requests. For example, if you want them to clean up their bedrooms, give them a time by which you'd like it done and stay out of their way until then. Letting children know that you believe they can meet their responsibilities without your hovering over them conveys positive regard for their ability and good will.

2. Don't condone unacceptable behavior when you believe your children are capable of doing what you expect. Otherwise, children will infer that you believe they can't do it.

3. Avoid baby talk. Talk to your children at a level which is more mature than the one they presently use. From time to time, introduce new vocabulary. Say what you want to say once rather than incessantly repeating yourself. Doing these things tells them that you have a high regard for their growing capacity for language comprehension and usage.

4. When children are unsuccessful in accomplishing something, tell them, "Maybe you can't do this today. But I bet you can do it soon." Don't take their actual accomplishments for granted. Praise them by saying, "Good going! I knew you could do it."

5. Ask your children how they feel about their strengths and weaknesses. Questions like, "Did you do as well as you wanted to?" or, "What would you do differently next time?" encourage children to engage in self-evaluation and let them know that you believe they can give themselves feedback and self-direction.

For Teachers:
1. Tell students that they can learn everything you'll be teaching them this school year. They learned to talk before ever coming to school and that is more difficult than anything they ever have to learn again.

2. Try to make your interactions with students as substantive and as educational as possible. Some students learn more just because their teachers try to teach more. Avoid spending a lot of time on instructions, managerial directions, or babbling.

3. Increase the length of time for *all* your students to respond to your questions. Teacher waiting time (the gap between the time you call on a student to answer a question and the time you talk again) of three to five seconds communicates a higher expectation that a student can respond successfully than a waiting time of one second. Research suggests that you will receive more responses and they will be longer, more thorough, and more confident.

4. Ask thought-provoking questions more than you do rote questions. The lower a teacher's expectations of students, the less students are asked to think and the more they are asked to simply remember. Questions which require students to analyze ("How can you tell . . . ?"), generalize ("How would you summarize . . . ?"), apply knowledge ("Give another example of . . .") or

speculate ("What might happen if . . . ?") are usually better than questions which require memorized, right-or-wrong information. 5. Develop similar ways to convey positive expectations about students' ability to behave properly in a classroom. Smile, touch, and tell students you'll keep trying to help them change their behavior.

Avoiding Labels

The opposite of being purveyors of positive expectations is to label children. Labeling children means to ascribe to them qualities which are overgeneralizing and unalterable: "This is my prize student." "This is the one who I send for a loaf of bread and doesn't come back." "This is my princess." "This one's my troublemaker." We label children because we want to preserve them just as they are and are afraid they may change; because we are so frustrated by their behavior and our ability to change it that we must convince ourselves that they cannot change; or because we can avoid taking responsibility for unresolved feelings about ourselves by attributing them to children.

When you find yourself repeatedly labeling a child, you can take this as an indication of overinvolvement. Your perception of the child is emotionally linked to your personal needs and thus, you may not see the child as he or she really is. As a result, your relationship with that child is knotted. The knot needs to be untangled a bit so there is some healthy distance between you and the child.

Here are some ways to avoid labeling:

- Start dealing with a labeled child incident by incident. Recognize when you use a negative incident as another piece of evidence in your desire to label the child. Try this experiment for one week: *Assume every time the child does something that concerns you that you are feeling the concern for the first time.* Deal with the present behavior assertively but don't link it to anything the child did before. If you keep doing this, we can almost guarantee that you will feel better about the child.

- Try to see the child from his or her perspective by the following role reversal experiment: *Imagine you are the child. Listen to your mother, father, teacher (whoever you really are to the child) talking to you. Remember a positive*

or negative message he or she frequently says to you that lets
you know how you are thought of, something which tells you
he or she sees you a certain way and insists that's the way you
are. Repeat the message in your head a few times. Now urge
that person to see you differently. Explain how you see your-
self and how you have been labeled unfairly. If you find
yourself unable to disagree with your parent or teacher, go
ahead and concede that he or she is right, but assert your
desire and ability to be different.

Reversing roles in this manner is difficult because your
perspective and the child's perspective has become quite
blurred. Keep trying this role reversal experiment until the
two perspectives become more distinct. To help you do this,
watch and listen closely to the child for clues about how he
or she sees things.

• A similar procedure for getting unhooked from the way you
see a labeled child is to confront yourself with these questions: What's repulsive about this child? What are the things
this child does that really unnerve and perhaps disgust you?
Are there other people who accept or even like these behaviors? Why? Do you secretly admire these behaviors? Are
these behaviors which you've struggled to stop in yourself?
What's attractive about this child? Is there anything about
the child you find interesting or compelling? Can you now
find more positive things about this child than you did before
considering these questions?

Giving Constructive Feedback

One of the major duties of an assertive parent or teacher is to
share reactions to children's behavior. As we get more satisfac-
torily involved with children, we can actually enhance our relationship by giving constructive feedback. Good feedback is like a
gift; it can bring us closer to children.

Below are guidelines for giving constructive feedback. Before
giving children feedback, check if your feedback meets these
criteria:

POTENTIAL OPENNESS OF THE CHILD

If at all possible, give feedback when there are indications the
child is potentially open to hear it. A child is usually not open if

we give the feedback in front of other children, or if the child is very involved in something else. Avoid negative feedback when the child has just lost face by a mistake or impulsive action (for example, has just broken something). We are often tempted to give criticism at a time the child is in the weakest position to receive it, but it is better to wait until the child is in a stronger position.

RECENT EVENTS

Although it is desirable at times to postpone giving feedback, the feedback should be given as close as possible to the time the event took place. Children, in particular, can have difficulty understanding the feedback if it is seriously delayed. For example, it is senseless to give detailed feedback concerning a child's musical performance a day later. The child's memory of the actual performance and the feelings associated with it may already be dimmed. This guideline of recent events also means staying focused on the recent behaviors in question. Remember to avoid bringing up old complaints in addition to the current ones (unless it is done to help clarify the present feedback).

DESCRIPTIVE, NOT INTERPRETIVE

Describing what a child has done and reporting its effect on others is much more helpful than reading into the child's motives. Saying things like, "I think you're just trying to get my attention" or, "You must be angry at someone else and you're taking it out on me" can be making unwarranted assumptions and inviting retaliation. It is better to say to the child, "Several times today, you interrupted other children when they were talking" than to say, "You think you always have something more important to say."

POSSIBLE TO CHANGE

Give feedback about behaviors a child can do something about. Children can be easily demoralized by remarks like, "You should be at fifth-grade level now" or, "You're awfully shy." It is better to suggest realistic, short-term goals than overnight, total changes. Telling the child, "I think you can stay with your homework ten more minutes tonight" is preferable to, "It's about time you really started doing a more thorough job on your school work." Finally, we have to be careful not to inundate the child with feedback; it's not possible for the child to change if given too many things to work on at once.

Finding a Balance Between Involvement and Detachment

Finding a reasonable balance between involvement and detachment is a constant challenge for parents and teachers. Sometimes a situation warrants closeness more than distance; or noninterference more than help; or challenge more than acceptance. To help you find the balance which is right for you, we offer these suggestions.

* *Give just enough support to children to help them get over a really tough hurdle without actually doing it for them.*

It is very hard for a parent or teacher to determine how much help to provide when a child is facing a lot of difficulty. Rescuing children from their problems is not helpful because they may never learn to cope with them alone. Sternly announcing that they must face the music is not the solution either. Children need adult support to feel that solving their own problems is worth it.

Here are some examples of support which stops short of rescue: Rather than taking over immediately, ask a young child if he wants help when he is having a tough time getting dressed by himself; review difficult homework assignments with a child but refuse to provide the answers; role play an anxious interpersonal situation with the child but insist that the child is on his own in the real encounter; provide some pros and cons for a difficult decision the child is facing but leave the actual decision to her.

* *Support children in activities they undertake of their own choosing. Give them the opportunity to succeed or fail on those choices.*

Children like to take on new challenges. Some examples are learning how a complicated toy works, mastering a musical instrument, trying out for a school play or athletic team, securing a job, or having a steady girlfriend or boyfriend. These interests may not always present the challenges we had in mind for our children. Nonetheless, they need our encouragement (providing they do not interfere with other responsibilities or could be harmful). In such situations, we need to watch out for three *red flags*.

The first red flag is our lack of interest in the child's initiative. We may feel, "Oh well, if that's what he thinks he should be doing now, it's his trip. It doesn't involve me. In my opinion, it's a waste of time." The problem arises because children of all ages benefit from the knowledge that their parents or teachers wish them well. If we fail to inquire how they are doing, or stay in touch with any of the problems they might incur, they will feel abandoned rather than wished well.

The second red flag is our urge to protect children, especially when we believe that they have bitten off more than they can chew. Taking responsibility for them at this point by doing too much for them or not permitting them to become more involved in the activity can be a big mistake. They need to learn from the natural consequences of their decisions and, using our best judgement, we need to let them risk as much failure as they can handle.

The third red flag is our need to take advantage of the child's initiative by becoming overly invested in it for a personal need. This can happen when adults try to show off their knowledge and skill to the child rather than help provide support. (For example, "Here's how this piano should sound" or, "Let me show you how to dribble that basketball.")

- *Be available to hear children's complaints but don't assume total responsibility for solving them.*

Some adults feel that children are one, big complaint department. To act out against this predicament, these adults dismiss children's complaints out of hand. Other adults feel intimidated by children's complaints and assume it's their job to patch up all situations so that the children are happy.

While adults cannot hear out children every time they bring up a complaint, it is helpful for children to know they can generally come to us with complaints (just as we want the same right with them). We are probably more receptive to listening if the complaints are expressed at times when we are not busy or at times which have deliberately been set aside to hear children's concerns, such as family or classroom meetings. Therefore, it is important to let children know *when* their complaints will get the best hearing. However, we should also allow for a tolerable level of complaining at inconvenient times in case there is some urgency.

It is also important to let children know *how* their complaints will get the best hearing. We should tell them and, if possible, demonstrate the way they can express themselves so that we will be most receptive to listening.

When listening to the complaints, we can avoid assuming full responsibility for solving them by asking questions such as:

- "What would be a better way to deal with this?"
- "Is there any way you can work this out for yourself?"
- "What can I do to help you now?"
- "What can we do so this doesn't happen again?"
- "Here is what I am willing to do about it . . . What will you do?"
- "Do you think I have total responsibility for what happened?"
- "This is what I suggest. Tell me what you think?"

A FINAL THOUGHT

It is our assumption that all of us are sufficiently imperfect to sometimes be disengaged or overinvolved in our relationships with children. Avoiding the dangers of either extreme is a realistic goal for all of us, but assuming we can achieve some mythical state of perfectly healthy involvement is not possible. What we're after is that mixture of involvement and detachment which enhances our assertiveness as parents and teachers. As long as we can approximate it, we have helped ourselves and our children considerably.

9 | Parents: Together and Alone

Many two-parent families are, for all intents and purposes, really one-parent families. That is, one parent is seen by the entire family as being in charge of the children. It is usually this parent who is the day-to-day disciplinarian, the reader of books on child rearing and the participant in parent-training workshops. Although one chief executive is useful and necessary in some organizations, families don't work efficiently unless both parents act as a team in the care and guiding of their children.

Like any organization, the family can be looked at as a system comprised of different subgroups. Some systems may include one parent and the children as one subgroup with the other parent as an outsider. Other systems may involve a close relationship between the parents and between the children but with little or no communication between these two subgroups. Families that develop sustained problems usually are ones where the boundaries between parents and children are not clear. The most effective family system is one in which the parents form one distinct and united subgroup and the children another with open channels of communication between them.

Even in our professional life, many of us have had to reckon with two bosses. One boss may align himself with the workers, while the other boss is left with the role of bad guy. On the other hand, if these two bosses talk to each other but not to the workers, the bosses may be shutting themselves off from valuable information. A more ideal situation might be two bosses who have a consistent way of dealing with workers and who also allow workers to freely express their views.

In the family unit, a consistent and flexible approach to parenting is often hard to achieve. When we ask parents whether they work as a team in dealing with their children, we sometimes get disheartening responses. For example:

- "We both want the marriage to work, so we don't talk about the kids because when we do, all we do is fight."
- "Ninety-five percent of our arguments are over the kids."
- "John and I need a mediator. We can't talk. We need a third party."
- "She makes me be the bad guy, but I think it's the other way around."
- "The kids have worked out a system of levels. They go first to their father and then to me."
- "He wants the kids to like him and goes easy on them in order to get that. The issue is who's going to be the bad guy."
- "His attitudes drive me more crazy than the children's behavior. I come down heavier on the kids as a result."
- "Our upbringings were very different. We have different ideas about child rearing."
- "We say we're going to compromise but never really do it."

Each set of responses above reflects an issue that may keep parents from developing a consistent approach to their children. The first issue is that many couples simply don't talk with each other about their children. Some fear seems to exist that such discussions might lead to fights and, potentially, threaten the marriage. Even when parents want to talk about the children, how to talk with each other productively seems to be the question.

A second issue that parents are painfully aware of is the effect that one partner's behavior toward the children can have on the other partner. None of us wants to be the bad guy. Consequently, we may vie with each other for favored-parent status. As a result, the authority of one of us may be undermined by the other. Or the responsibility for the children can be pushed from one parent to the other. The proverbial "Wait till your father gets home" epitomizes this avoidance of responsibility. We know that we and our children are negatively affected by such situations and none of us consciously wants to encourage children to play one parent against the other. What is needed is an atmosphere in which both parents can feel in charge and supported by their spouse and their children.

Couples also seem to be very conscious of the fact that consistent discipline is seriously threatened by a lack of agreement between them. Two people usually have some differing views about child rearing because of their different experiences. This makes communication particularly difficult and especially crucial because if parents are to work together, important differences must be reconciled. Being responsible about our relationship with children as well as our marital relationship is a difficult task. Some people see it as having to choose between two love relationships —their children or their spouse.

In summary, being assertive with children is not enough. We must risk being assertive with each other as well. Assertion, in this case, means talking about attitudes toward child rearing; coming to basic agreements about how to deal with the children; respecting each other's differences; and developing a team approach to parenting.

There are several ways to facilitate communication about children with our partner. Some of the following ideas are taken from the assertion literature which focuses on adult-to-adult communication. We have also added strategies specific to couples trying to deal with children as a team. The goals of effective communication between parents are twofold: (1) to clearly communicate our attitudes, wants and plans to our spouse in an effort to foster a relatively harmonious approach to parenting; and (2) to jointly discuss and plan for the problems, needs, and disciplining of our children.

STICKING TO THE ISSUE

Sometimes a simple discussion about a child's behavior can quickly escalate into a marital feud. For example:

Father: I don't like it when Mary stays out too late.
Mother: Neither do I.

Father:	But I'm usually not here when she's leaving. Why don't you remind her to be home on time?
Mother:	How do you know whether I remind her or not? In fact, I do remind her. But you never say anything to her about it even when you are home—which isn't often!
Father:	You know I have to work late a lot. How can I feed all of us if I don't? What do you want from me?
Mother:	A little support, that's all.
Father:	You get support from me—my paycheck!
Mother:	I don't want to feel like the raising of *our* children is *my* responsibility. I want your help, too.
Father:	Everytime we talk about the kids we end up fighting. This is ridiculous! I'm going to sleep!

When discussion ensues over problems with the children, the biggest energy-drainer is speaking past the issue at hand. Failure to stick to the issue inevitably leads to escalation and conflict. In the preceding example, the issue—Mary's lateness—was forgotten and another issue—Father's lack of support for Mother—led to an argument. Energy is saved if we focus directly on the problem at hand and help our partner to do so as well. When either party speaks past the issue, the discussion gets sidetracked. It takes that much longer to resolve the problem, if it is resolved at all.

The first step to take in helping you and your spouse keep to the issue is to identify how each of you typically gets the discussion off track. Becoming aware of your sidetracking behaviors enables you to stop yourself in the heat of a conflict and return to the issue at hand; gaining recognition of your partner's sidetracking behaviors enables you to help him or her stay with the issue. Some of the ways that adults speak past the issue are:

- taking offense at *how* your partner is talking to you ("How dare you talk to me in that tone of voice!")
- bringing up other complaints ("I also don't like it when you . . .")
- challenging every argument that's presented ("How can you say that . . . ?")
- giving excuses ("I had such a hard day at work.")
- feeling hurt ("You don't care about how I feel.")

The next time you find yourself in a dispute, listen for some of these tactics which get the discussion off beam. Perhaps you will find yourself speaking past the issue. Maybe you will hear your partner doing so. Or, possibly, you'll discover that both of you are speaking past each other, like two ships passing in the night. At the moment that any of these realizations hit you, stop the discussion and insist: "Wait a minute! I want to figure out how we're going to solve the problem we have right now." This move freezes the action between you and allows you to refocus.

In his book, *When I Say No, I Feel Guilty,* Manuel Smith suggested *fogging* as another way to keep the discussion focused. It simply means accepting your partner's feelings and refocusing the discussion in order to avoid the escalation of conflict. For example:

Father: I don't like it when Mary stays out too late.
Mother: Neither do I.
Father: But I'm not usually here when she's leaving. Why don't you remind her to be home on time?
Mother: How do you know whether I remind her or not? In fact, I do remind her. But you never say anything to her about it even when you are home—which isn't often.
Father: You're right, I'm not home as much as I'd like to be. But right now let's figure out what to do with Mary.
Mother: Well, I tell her but she doesn't seem to listen to me.
Father: Would it help if we both talk to her?
Mother: Yes, I think so. I don't want to feel like it's just my job.
Father: I may sometimes give you the impression that it's your job but it's our job. Let's sit down with Mary tomorrow. What exactly do we want to get across to her?

During the discussion, there were a few opportunities to get sidetracked. For instance, when Mother said, "You never say anything to her even when you are home—which isn't often," Father could have become angry and the discussion might have become a fight, as in the first example. The original issue might have gotten lost in a flurry of accusations and defensive statements. Fogging helps to avoid this escalation from a discussion to a battle.

We should be aware, however, that fogging involves some risks. It may keep us from listening to something important that our partner is saying. It can also be used to discount what our spouse says. In the previous dialogue, for example, the father did not ignore the mother's feelings. His last statement probably made it easier for both of them to rationally discuss Mary's behavior. Used sparingly, and in the interest of avoiding a useless battle, fogging can be an effective aid to communication.

AVOIDING THE MIDDLE MAN

In our heart of hearts, most of us want our children to love us more than anyone else—maybe even more than our partner. This is a fairly natural reaction but one that can cause problems for us, our spouse, and our children. If we're angry with our spouse, we may vent our frustrations in the children's presence in such a way that we look good and our partner looks bad. Statements like, "Your father's never here when I need him," or, "It's fine with *me* if you go to the party," are usually said in anger. They have the effect, however, of pitting one parent against the other in children's eyes. Such statements are also indirect. That is, instead of directly confronting our partner with gripes and concerns, we tell the children. Children can't do anything about conflicts between their parents but implicitly may feel that they should arbitrate their parents' conflicts.

When there are conflicts between us, it is imperative to talk with each other directly rather than through the children. Confronting our partner directly may feel less frightening if we believe we have the skills to do so effectively. When you communicate your reactions toward your partner in a descriptive, nonjudgmental way, the discussion is more likely to be productive. "You're just a pushover with the kids," is not easy to hear without becoming defensive and argumentative. It also conveys your dissatisfaction and anger but does not tell your partner exactly what behavior you are dissatisfied with. Discussion in previous chapters has focused on clear, direct communications. In the same ways that these messages facilitate communication with children, they can help us say what we want to say to our partner —and be heard.

When you are the recipient of a general negative statement

such as, "I don't like the way you deal with the children," you can also help yourself get more descriptive feedback by asking your partner to be more specific about the complaint. For example:

Father: I don't like the way you deal with the children.
Mother: What is it that I do that you don't like?
Father: Everything!
Mother: Something's really bothering you and I'd like to know what it is.
Father: Like tonight at dinner—Don didn't want to eat what we'd cooked, so you made him something else.
Mother: You don't want me to make special orders for Don?
Father: No. He has to learn to eat different kinds of food, don't you think?
Mother: Sometimes I forget he's not a baby anymore. I think you're right. I shouldn't be doing that. OK, what else do I do with the kids that bothers you?
Father: That's really all that was on my mind, I guess.
Mother: I'm glad we talked. I thought you were really mad at me.
Father: I was. But I'm not anymore.

This approach helps communication in two ways. First, it enables us to find out what the specific problem really is and, second, it helps us evaluate the feedback and decide if we want to change our behavior or not.

If you and your partner still disagree, compromise can be attempted. The previous dialogue might have gone this way:

Mother: You don't want me to make special orders for Don?
Father: No. He has to learn to eat different kinds of food.
Mother: But he's not old enough yet. I think it would be too much to force him to eat everything he doesn't like.
Father: We have to begin somewhere.
Mother: I suppose.
Father: Maybe we could start with just a couple of foods.
Mother: I guess we could try that.

Because of the different ways that people are raised, parents are very likely to have differing views of the best approach to raising their own children. Rather than facing this reality, one parent often bows out, leaving the other in charge of what's best. But when this happens, the parent who bows out usually winds up feeling uninvolved and may even undercut the other's methods. Or the two parents may exaggerate their differences in ways that confuse children. For example, the father may be more lax than the mother about discipline. To provoke the father, the mother may intensify her sternness, which precipitates even greater permissiveness on the part of the father. A small difference thus begins to look like the Grand Canyon.

Compromise helps us to bridge our differences and to develop a consistent, supportive approach in which both parents are able to get some of what they want. A plan derived through compromise is often a better plan because both parents are more likely to be committed to seeing that it works. But it is often difficult to convince one or both parents of this truth because they have not given sufficient thought to what options for compromise exist for them in a particular conflict. Therefore, it is especially important that the couple generate as many possible solutions to an impasse between them before they decide if a meaningful compromise exists.

Naturally, compromise isn't possible or even desirable when our individual beliefs are very strong. To concede in such situations could feel like a threat to our personal integrity. Religious views, dating, and corporal punishment are just a few of the possible areas of unresolvable conflicts. While these impasses are terribly difficult, some of them can be transformed into powerful learning experiences for both parents and children.

If one parent feels more strongly than the other about an issue, it may make sense to let that person's wishes predominate. However, we need to be careful not to give up our rights too easily. If both parents are deeply committed to opposing values, they each have the right to hold these beliefs. In such situations, open discussion between the parents about the conflict is necessary. A joint commitment to respect each other's wishes is needed as well.

In one family, for instance, the mother felt strongly that teenagers should never be allowed to drink. The father, however, felt that occasional drinking, in moderation, would help the children learn to use alcohol appropriately. After much conflict, they opened themselves to several alternatives and then decided that no drinking would be permitted when the mother was around. They also agreed that under no circumstances would unsupervised use of alcohol be allowed, but the father could have an occasional drink with the teen-agers when the mother was out. The parents explained their differences and the plan to the children. In this way, the values of both parents were respected and the conflict was at least partially resolved.

It is important for children to learn that people don't always agree on everything. Demonstrating acceptance and respect for each other's views can help children learn tolerance of individual differences. Children can also benefit from knowing that there is more than one approach to an issue. What could be an area of intense conflict can become a mechanism for teaching a vitally important value—individual human rights.

ADVANCE PLANNING

To develop a team approach to dealing with children, partners need to set aside time to discuss strategies for dealing with each child. Frequently, our work, the dishes, baseball games, bills, and errands take precedence over this necessary planning time. Because most of us discuss our children only in times of crisis, we're often reactive rather than proactive. Lack of advance planning makes it difficult to make and enforce rules and to deal with the changes in our children as they grow older. Taking the time for advance planning will save time in the long run; being prepared to deal with situations as they arise ultimately saves energy.

Steps in a planning session might include comparing observations of a particular child's behavior, deciding what particular behaviors you want to work on, looking at how you've been responding to these behaviors in the past, developing a strategy to address these behaviors, and deciding how long you will try the strategy before you review the situation again to see if the plan is working.

RAISING CHILDREN ALONE

Many of the issues we've raised so far are relevant to single parents. However, there are other concerns that are unique to adults that are raising children alone. As the number of single parents has grown, so has the number of resource books devoted solely to this topic. Because we cannot comprehensively address the needs of single parents here, we refer the reader to books on this topic in the *Further Reading* section at the end of this book.

There are, however, three key suggestions that we find important to mention.

Build a Support System.

Sometimes a single parent will say, "I'm on my own. There's no one to take over for a while and there's no one to check things out with." For individuals raising children alone, feelings of isolation and lack of support from other adults are sources of tension. There are, however, other adults in your environment that will be helpful to you—if you let them. Relatives, friends, other single parents, your ex-partner, and your children are all potential supports for you.

We suggest that you *directly* ask them for their ongoing assistance with the problems you face as a single parent. Here are some possible ways to express to others your need for their continuing support:

- "Sometimes I need to get away from the kids for a while. It might be for an evening or for a day or two. When that happens, I'd like to be able to leave the children with someone who cares about them and about me. If I need to do that, I'd like to know that I could ask you and that you would do it, if you could."
- "When I'm confused about what to do with the kids, I'd like to be able to come over and talk with you about the situation. It helps me clarify my thinking if I can talk to someone like you."
- "We're all single parents. I thought it might be a good idea to meet on a regular basis to discuss our concerns. What do you think?"

Deal With Your Guilt

We've frequently heard single parents say things like, "I feel guilty about not providing a normal home life for the children" or, "I have to work if we're going to eat, but I know that the kids feel deprived. I feel like I have to make up for that."

Guilt about not providing the ideal home environment can lead to superhuman efforts to make up for this loss to our children. We may spoil children, try to be mother and father, and attempt to be the perfect parent in order to reduce our own feelings of guilt.

There are other ways to deal with guilt that may help us to avoid spoiling children or expecting too much of ourselves. One way to reduce guilt feelings is to disclose them. Talk honestly to your children about the change your family has experienced without using this as an opportunity to vent your frustrations. Give them as much information as they need to understand what has happened. Share your feelings about being a single parent without overwhelming the children or making them feel that the situation is in any way their fault. Accept the children's feelings of loss, anger, or deprivation without letting their feelings control your actions. Answer questions about what happened to the family as objectively as possible.

Communicate With Your "Ex"

If your ex-partner is involved in some way with the children, conflicts may naturally develop. Some single parents tell us, "Sometimes the kids get caught between my ex and myself" or, "He takes them for the weekend and spoils them to death. I've got them the rest of the time and try to be firm, and appear to be the villain."

It may be possible, however, to rely on your ex as a consultant and co-parent. It is true that it is much more difficult to work as a team when parents don't have the same residence. Many single parents have hostile feelings toward their ex-spouse and try, sometimes inadvertently, to turn the children away from their other parent. But it is also true that children may feel torn when their parents say negative things about each other. The favorite parent syndrome can be a continuation of the conflict that led to the initial separation, but now the fight is conducted through the children. The children don't necessarily share these hostilities, and usually want an ongoing relationship with both parents. Efforts need to be made, therefore, to facilitate communication between the parents in order to maintain a sense of stability for the children.

The same communication skills discussed for two-parent families will help to establish a consistent approach between you and your children's other parent. Time to do this, however, is limited by the fact that you're not in constant contact with each other. The first task, may be to negotiate times when you will discuss your children, work out some of your differences of opinion about child rearing, and develop, as much as possible, consistent plans.

We have used one- and two-parent families to describe some ways to communicate with the adults in your family system. The suggestions given in this chapter can be applied to other kinds of families as well—foster parents and step parents. For example, these ideas can be used to deal with the natural parents of your foster child. The key is to be as assertive with the adults in your children's lives as you are with your children. Assertion with children is important but cannot be maximally effective unless we are also assertive with each other.

10 | It's Different in the Classroom

Until recently, it was fashionable for educators to proclaim that the problem of classroom discipline did not exist. As long as the curriculum was relevant and instruction individualized, any major nuisance could be prevented. Now there is a growing recognition that *every* classroom has a heavy dose of behavior problems that arise despite the instructional planning that has been undertaken. As a result, it has become increasingly acceptable to help teachers cope directly with discipline problems.

Numerous books and articles have appeared in the last few years which offer concrete advice on discipline. In-service workshops related to the practical art of classroom management have also proliferated. We see this book as part of the effort to grapple directly with student misbehavior. It is our hope that those of you who are teachers have benefited from the ideas and suggestions so far.

Until now, we have treated you no differently than we have readers who are parents. We did so because the issues and ideas we have raised are as relevant to you as they are to parents. But there are some respects in which your attempt to create an assertive authority role with children is dissimilar from the process parents must undergo. It *is* different in the classroom.

Even though this chapter is specially geared to teaching, we hope that parent readers will not skip it. The partnership between parents and teachers is absolutely critical to the continuity of assertive authority in children's lives. Parents need to understand and support the ways in which teachers are able to assert themselves with their children. Reading this chapter will be one small way in which parents can be of help.

HOW CLASSROOM GROUPS DIFFER FROM FAMILIES

There are five major differences between classroom life and family life that have special consequences for a teacher's exercise of authority.*

1. Classrooms are crowded places. Typically, more than twenty children coexist for most of their activity in one room. Usually, only one adult is there to supervise them. The average family, on the other hand, operates in more than one room and the adult-to-child ratio is far lower. Therefore, the potential for incidents requiring adult control and restriction is much greater in classrooms. Moreover, if children choose to ally themselves against the teacher's authority, they can muster a larger army than a group of siblings ever can. Teachers are also more hassled because of these crowded conditions. They tend to have up to 500 more daily interactions with children than parents do.

2. A classroom presents little opportunity for privacy. Many events occurring there are carried out aloud and in front of everybody. If teachers want to counsel a child who is experiencing a problem or work through a conflict with one student privately, they have little time and space to do so. Furthermore, the misbehavior of one child can have a contagious effect as classmates observe what the child is doing and decide to join in the fun. As every adult has experienced, a child's leverage is much greater in public places, from supermarkets to classrooms.

3. Teachers cannot draw upon an intimate and prolonged relationship with children to establish their goodwill. While it is true that teachers can develop close bonds with their students, they do

---

*For a fascinating and more extensive look at how classrooms and families differ, see Robert Dreeben, *On What is Learned in Schools,* (Reading, Mass.: Addison-Wesley, 1968).

not have nearly as many emotional resources to support their authority role as parents enjoy. Because teachers have a more difficult time developing a personal connection with children, their authority can be more easily dismissed by children. In particular, the withdrawal of affection on the part of a teacher has significantly less impact than would parental rejection of a child.

4. *There are few means to punish students in school.* Classroom teachers dispense few privileges that can be denied as a disciplinary measure. Parents, by contrast, can withhold TV, food treats, allowance, and other goodies. Likewise, the removal of a child from ongoing classroom activity is much harder to implement than is a child's removal from a family activity. Some teachers even find, to their dismay, that removal from classroom activity is often relished by students.

5. *A teacher's authority can be easily undermined by parents and administrators.* Parents can pretty much do what they want with their children, but teachers are subject to intense public scrutiny. Whenever parents or administrators disagree with the actions of a teacher, political pressure can be brought to bear to change them (even though some protections are granted by teacher contracts). On a more subtle basis, parents and administrators can demean teachers in front of children and thereby affect children's respect for teacher authority.

Taken together, these five aspects of classroom life present teachers with a difficult challenge. If they want to actively assert their authority, they have to find ways to overcome these obstacles or must act in spite of them. Although we believe that this challenge can be met, we can certainly empathize with the hopelessness many teachers feel. We continually meet teachers who are leaving the profession because they find their jobs untenable. Chief among their reasons for seeking a new career is that coping with large numbers of students is a hell they were not trained to handle or given support to endure.

HOW TEACHERS CAN GET SUPPORT

Because of the obstacles we have noted, we are convinced that teachers cannot assertively take charge of their classrooms all by themselves. They need the support of others—students, fellow teachers, parents, and administrators—to overcome the odds facing them. The problem is that these sources of support cannot be taken for granted. Teachers need to actively seek the goodwill and backup help they require. The question is how?

Teachers as Group Leaders

In our opinion, the most effective way for teachers to gain students' support for their authority is to establish themselves as the *group leader* of their classroom. We choose this term to denote those functions a teacher performs to regulate and solidify the interpersonal relations among students. These actions include such things as helping students to like and respect each other, to share their ideas and feelings, to harmonize destructive differences of opinion, and to simply enjoy working and being together. We stress these functions because teachers cannot survive for long with an orientation that only treats children individually. The classroom group as a whole is an important entity which a teacher must guide.

Not realizing this, some teachers try to gain tight control by keeping students away from each other as much as possible. If they attempt to keep students at arm's length, however, teachers usually give themselves trouble. We once observed, for example, a junior high school teacher who tried to avoid discipline problems by placing desks far apart, assigning boys to odd numbered rows and girls to even numbered rows. Although the students were initially held under control by this seating arrangement, it did not take long for them to find ways to make life miserable for the teacher.

The student group, by its sheer size alone, is potentially more powerful than the teacher can ever be. If the teacher does not respect this potentiality and instead imposes severe restrictions on student interaction, he or she is begging for retaliation. The teacher is much better off working to develop a strong sense of community in the classroom. This goal is well worth the effort for an additional reason. As any teacher knows, a sizable percentage of student misbehavior stems from tensions in the peer group. If the teacher can help this group become a friendly haven for its members, many discipline problems can be averted. When the peer group is cohesive, the teacher is not continually forced to assume the burden of keeping individual students in line. The students themselves can help each other behave.

To develop an effective group, a teacher's first task is to find ways to make the total group attractive to its members. Many classroom groups suffer from the problems of divisive cliques, infrequent interaction between boys and girls, and students who are simply afraid of group membership. These problems affect the students' well-being and the teacher's ability to maintain leadership of the group. One way to help students find the group attractive is to include at the beginning of the school year (and reintroduce later on when needed) fun-filled group building activities.* Here are some brief examples:

- *Name Chain.* With the group seated in a circle, a first person states his name, the second person states both his name and the person's name before him, etc. until the last person (preferably the teacher) states the names of all the children in the circle along with her own.
- *Name Bingo.* Each person writes down on a bingo card the names of all his classmates in any order or arrangement; the group then proceeds to play bingo using names instead of numbers.
- *Human Scavenger Hunt.* A sheet is prepared for each student with instructions to find classmates who have specific characteristics: Who has blue eyes? Who has a birthday in the winter? Who likes science fiction?
- *Class Information List.* A large poster is placed on display listing the skills, interests, hobbies, etc. of class members; the information is gleaned from interviews students have with each other. The poster can also include vital facts about the class such as the total weight, height, and age of all the students combined.
- *Group Cohesion Experiences.* These are activities to give a class a sense of identity and pride (for example, writing a class newspaper, designing a class T-shirt, constructing a leisure reading area, etc.).

Another way to build group attraction and cohesion is to encourage students from the start to share knowledge and help each

*See Gene Stanford, *Developing Effective Classroom Groups: A Practical Guide for Teachers*, (New York: Hart Publishing Co., 1977) for an extensive collection of activities.

other. This encouragement can be given by simply asking students to get help from their classmates before they seek the teacher's assistance. Group projects, joint papers, peer tutoring, and student-led discussion groups can lend this encouragement as well.

An interesting experiment a fourth-grade teacher tried for one month (we imagine it could last longer for older students) was the use of arithmetic groups. After dividing her students into groups of four, she asked each group to designate its members A, B, C, or D. A was Monday, B was Tuesday, C was Wednesday, and D was Thursday. On Monday night, student A designed a set of arithmetic problems for B, C, and D and checked with an adult to see that his answers were correct. The next morning, A presented his problems to the group and then the group worked on them with A giving assistance and checking answers. This patterns repeated itself with B, C, and D. The following Monday each group of four designed their own mastery test on the previous week's work and then took its own test. During the week, any problems that the students had which could not be solved by the student teachers were presented to the classroom teacher. On some occasions, the teacher even had to help the entire group, but at least the problem was one common to all the children in that group. When the teacher thought the entire class was ready for a mastery test, she administered it herself.

A similar experiment was conducted by a highly regarded high school typing instructor who was perplexed by how to inspire a roomful of thirty restless students (some of whom were there only because they had to be) to type well. One idea the teacher had was to arrange desks in ten groups of three. This set up the possibility of a joint proofreading process in which the students check their own work, then move to the other two typists' seats to check their work. By the time the students have returned to their typewriters, the work has been proofread three times, thus ensuring a better accuracy grade for all involved.

The teacher was also surprised by the heightened interest this new seating arrangement created. She wrote: "I honestly anticipated some disciplinary situations as a result of moving the desks closer together, but so far the students have shown a remarkable sense of courtesy toward each other. They are quite willing, with no urging from me, to help each other work out problems they run into in the course of typing an assignment. The problem of trying to bring a student who has been absent up-to-date on classwork, while also trying to work with the rest of the class, has virtually solved itself. Students are more willing to volunteer some of their time to show those who have been out what they missed, realizing that they are still responsible for their own assignment."

As students feel comfortable with each other and have been encouraged to help and share, a teacher can increase the degree to which small and large group activities occur in the classroom routine. It's useful to discuss with students what makes for good and poor group behavior and to ask them to evaluate how they are doing when working together in a group. The teacher needs to curb any tendency at this point to preach about social virtues. If the teacher does not like what's going on among the students in a group or in the whole class, he should tell them his concerns in a truthful but sensitive manner and ask students for suggestions to make things better. One mechanism for doing this is to form a class steering committee whose membership rotates every two weeks and invite it to recommend guidelines for improving small group and large group effectiveness.

As the year progresses, a teacher must continually let students know that she is really interested in the group's well-being. Every opportunity to show students what a group can accomplish and how belonging to it can give everyone a good feeling should be utilized.

Whether or not a teacher is group-oriented, there is still a strong possibility that destructive competition or social exclusion will occur among students. When this happens, the sense of well-being in a classroom can break down. There are several interventions a teacher can make to stop such a pattern before it is too late: airing the problem with the class; taking direct action to separate cliques of students who tyrannize others; or structuring more learning tasks which demand cooperative behavior.*

These interventions will succeed to the extent that the teacher has gained respect from students for her skills as a group leader. Based on research studies about group leadership and student attitudes, we have identified four basic skills that students want

---

*For help on these interventions, see David W. Johnson and Roger T. Johnson, *Learning Together and Alone: Cooperation, Competition and Individualization,* (Englewood Cliffs: Prentice-Hall, 1975).

group-oriented teachers to possess. The more one has of these, the stronger one's influence among students is likely to be.

1. *Be a Stimulator.* This is the ability to energize a class. Even if low-key, as long as the teacher is an interesting person to the students and can provide challenging and exciting learning activities, students will be energized to work hard. A teacher who also appeals to students' personal concerns is likely to arouse even more heightened interest. A stimulating teacher is also given less trouble than a teacher who bores students.

2. *Be a Supporter.* This is the ability to communicate to a class that they are cared about as individuals and as a class. One of the basic caring gestures is to simply talk to students on a friendly, nonacademic basis whenever the opportunity presents itself. In addition, if the class is restless, support can be shown when a teacher adjusts demands and finds ways to make learning experiences nonthreatening. When support is given to students, a class is more likely to return the support to the teacher and to each other.

3. *Be a Meaning-maker.* This is the ability to help students make sense out of their school experiences. Students often feel that they don't know what's happening in school. They don't know why they are taught certain material, or how their learning from one subject to another interrelates. A teacher also helps a class to get meaning from school by connecting new learning to the students' experiences *out* of school and to their existing classroom knowledge.

4. *Be a Manager.* This is the ability to develop well-organized procedures for the movement of students and work. Students dislike teachers who make them wait a lot, who interrupt lessons to handle minor disturbances, who give confusing instructions, and who don't provide sufficient information about upcoming events. When teachers eliminate such disruptions, their prestige in the eyes of students is appreciably enhanced.

With such skills, group-oriented teachers are also able to gain acceptance for their own decisions about managing the classroom. *All teachers need the prerogative to establish long-term rules and policies to regulate student performance and behavior.* As any teacher soon learns, every conflict can't be solved spontaneously. It is impossible to always deal on-the-spot with uncompleted homework, forgotten milk money, or missing worksheets. Students need to know in advance what happens when these things occur. Otherwise, teachers are forced to adjudicate every situation that arises and thus will never be able to complete their instructional responsibilities. It behooves teachers to anticipate what can go wrong and to create standardized methods for dealing with problems so the classroom can run more smoothly. It is fair to say that teachers have to be far more efficiency-minded than parents do.

Consistent procedures for coping with misbehavior are especially important. The teacher's mood should not dictate a response to unacceptable behavior because that only leads to permissiveness some days and harshness on other days. The metaphor of a referee who objectively administers penalties to infractions was used in chapter 6 to describe the stance of an *assertive penalizer*. This metaphor is particularly useful to guide teachers' actions in a classroom. For example, a teacher could institute a standard *three chance plan* for dealing with rule breaking. The first infraction might be handled by the teacher stating the unacceptable behavior and explaining why it is unacceptable. The second infraction could be a warning that the child will be penalized if the behavior occurs again. The third infraction could bring an automatic penalty (detention, for example). We have found that when students know that the teacher will consistently react this way to misbehavior, discipline problems diminish and the teacher's authority role is enhanced. Whether this particular procedure will work for you depends on your classroom situation, but the point is that some systematic way of dealing with misbehavior is needed. Students want their leader to be predictable, fair, and strong.

Collaborating With Other Teachers

The second critical source of support for teachers is each other. When teachers work together to solve disciplinary problems, there is a far better chance that they can assert their authority effectively. Let's look at some of the ways teacher collaboration pays off.

The simplest form of collaboration is to swap ideas for handling classroom management problems. Residing within any school faculty are countless strategies, techniques, and skills which often remain unknown to the whole staff. Usually teachers, confronted with their own problems, use their own experiences to create solutions which they keep to themselves. When this happens, there is an incredible waste of the rich, natural resources within a faculty. Some teachers, for example, have figured out a few standard penalties for student misbehavior which deter further misbehavior without disrupting the activities of the rest of the class. Other teachers have been skillful at physically arranging the contents of their classroom so that students can move about and get supplies without bumping into each other, loitering, or fighting. Still other teachers are adept at avoiding power struggles with defiant students. It's a pity when this knowledge is not shared.

In some schools, there is not only little swapping of disciplinary strategies, but also a reluctance to give or seek help of any kind. Instead, teachers generally keep to themselves and use the teacher's lounge for anything but shop talk. This phenomenon occurs, no doubt, because teachers work in isolation from each other and see each other very little during the course of the school day. Matters become worse when this physical isolation breeds suspicion and distrust.

It usually requires some assertive act by a courageous teacher to overcome these obstacles. A first step taken by one teacher we know was to speak up at faculty meetings about her conviction that the faculty needed more professional exchange. When she aroused some interest, she followed with a suggestion to set aside ten minutes at the beginning of each meeting for teachers to form small groups and voluntarily share (without group reaction) any successes or problems they had in the area of discipline. The suggestion was accepted and carried out. This initial strategy was meant to facilitate awareness that other teachers have problems and successes as well and to encourage exchange and reaction at a later time. The strategy was successful. From this simple start, trust and interest grew to the extent that six months later, two entire faculty meetings were devoted to swapping experiences, ideas, and suggestions. In addition, several teachers began calling each other on the phone to give and receive advice. The teachers were amazed by how much they had to give each other.

A second way for teachers to collaborate is to identify joint actions which could make each teacher's job of managing students easier and more effective. In many schools, for example, teachers have gotten together and with the input of students, parents, and administrators have created a joint discipline code. The most important function these discipline codes play is to *clearly describe* those behaviors which are encouraged or discouraged in the general school community. Having this information in writing helps students become more aware of their responsibility to others. Disseminating discipline code booklets to parents gives them the information upon which to support the school's efforts with discipline.

Another joint action is for teachers to develop a coordinated plan for keeping corridor traffic under control, for supervising recess activities, or for maintaining student decorum in school assemblies. Believing that it is the school principal's job to figure out these plans, some teachers balk at this form of collaboration. Yet in our experience, we have seen that when teachers assume active responsibility for solving such problems, the solutions are more likely to both receive everyone's support and bring permanent results. For example, we learned about teachers in an urban junior high school who, despite their principal's instructions to monitor student behavior in the hallway, would literally closet themselves in their classrooms between periods while students produced mayhem in the corridors. The teachers, it seemed, did not trust that they would get help from each other if a rough confrontation with students occurred. As a result, no one participated in the monitoring assignment. Fortunately, with support from outside consultants, they aired their distrust and worked out a plan to eliminate the hallway disturbances. The plan worked because they all supported it.

Another kind of action was taken by an urban elementary school faculty. After months of complaining to each other about how restless students became when the weather was bad, some teachers got the idea to let students visit other classrooms on rainy days. It took some creative thinking to work out the logistics and ground rules of the plan and to convince the principal of its merit, but, once achieved, the plan went into action and worked beautifully.

Another avenue of collaboration is for teachers to meet together, with the guidance of a school counselor, and plan how to help a troubled student with whom they each have contact. Such collaboration is appropriate in elementary schools where team teaching is practiced, or where gym, art, science, and music teachers exist in addition to the regular classroom teacher. Beyond elementary school, this collaboration is particularly helpful because it is common practice for a student to have several teachers. Once together, these teachers can share perceptions of the child's difficulties, brainstorm all the ways the student might be helped, and select a plan of action which has the most promise.

There may be reluctance to participate in such a process but most teachers who have given it a try have come away deeply impressed by the strength of collaborative planning. Not only do creative solutions emerge, but the actual implementation of the chosen plan succeeds, no doubt because of the support of several people. For example, a high school student with a 125 IQ was a source of concern to her teachers because she was doing failing work, even in classes geared to students with low academic ability. When the teachers met with a school counselor, they decided to move her to a higher academic track, hoping the confidence shown in her ability would be a positive influence. They also worked out a plan for how the student would be told about their action. Although the student was initially annoyed by the plan, the teachers remained encouraging and within two weeks, the student was holding her own with the new academic expectations and taking a more active interest in school.

Parents as Partners

Frequently (and sometimes for good reason), teachers consider parents to be as much of a nuisance as their children. Parents are known to complain about almost anything: the homework given by the teacher is too little (or too much); the learning process in school is too unstructured (or too structured); their children (or other parents' kids) are not disciplined enough. To keep parents out of their hair, some teachers find it best to keep contact to a minimum. But if the parents are sufficiently aggressive, the teacher hears from them anyway and finds herself on the defensive.

Teachers do better when they make active efforts to include parents. In dealing with parents, it is particularly important to dispel from the start any feelings that the teacher is the parent's adversary, and replace it with the hope that their relationship will be a partnership. When teachers succeed in this task, they can get the parental support needed to back up their authority role.

A way for a teacher to begin is to inform parents as soon as possible about the nature of his or her program, any special plans that have been made for the school year, and the kinds of expectations he or she has for students and parents. A fourth-grade teacher, for example, was really intent on motivating students to write. He let parents know about his stress on writing skills in an informal letter sent home in the first few weeks of school. He mentioned in the letter his hope to create a simulated publishing company in the classroom and his intention to ask students to write at least one poem, short story, or feature article a week. The letter concluded with suggestions of how parents could support his efforts. Too often teachers have goals, plans, and expectations that parents could effectively support if they knew about them in advance and if they were asked to reinforce them at home. The only way parents frequently hear about the teacher's program is through their children's report, which can be distorted.

Many school rules and regulations are especially important for parents to know about. An obvious example is the practice of many schools to have children obtain their parents' signature on graded work done by the child. Sometimes parents are not told about such a rule and its rationale. What typically happens is that the child sheepishly presents the paper to his or her parents and mutters something like, "Here. You're supposed to sign this." Taken by surprise, parents may not be as receptive to this procedure as the teacher would hope. Similarly, parents are often confused by their children's account of the kinds of school supplies they are to purchase. Parents would be helped to have a supply list sent home with their children.

Another way to include parents is to send a newsletter home periodically, describing recent happenings in the classroom. Included could be information on what the class is studying, what special activities have taken place, and comments of appreciation to parents who have assisted the teacher. This idea is almost always appreciated and helps to establish trust and confidence in parents.

Most elementary schools (and some higher schools) have back to school nights or an open house for parents early in the school year. At these times, parents meet their children's teachers and receive a firsthand report of what a child experiences in the classrooms. Often, these events have a ritualistic feel to them and fail to inspire any meaningful level of parental support. One alternative to this usually humdrum affair is to invite children to join their parents for the program and enlist them to show parents around the classroom. This can be followed by some activities that parents and children do together. One teacher, for example, arranged a series of science experiments which both parties enjoyed doing.

Probably the best opportunity teachers have to gain parental support is the teacher-parent conference. The first time parents and teachers meet privately, it is appropriate to use the conference to hear the parents' observations about their child. Parents can be asked, for example, to relate the child's interests as they see them and to indicate the needs, habits, and self-attitudes the child shows at home which might reflect on the school performance. A teacher may learn from parents, for example, that a child feels inferior to an older sibling because the latter has always done better in school or has more easily established a close relationship with the parents. Armed with such information, the teacher can then invite parents to help plan how to maximize the child's feelings of self-worth in school.

If the teacher has already developed concerns about the child, they should not be held back. Parents are less defensive if the concerns are stated directly and clearly. When parents have been dealt with honestly, they often respond with useful insights. For example, a teacher said to a first-grader's parents, "I'm worried about Patrick. He seems to tune out whenever I give him instructions." After some hesitation, Patrick's parents reported that the same thing happens at home and offered the thought that perhaps he does this because they don't listen and respond to him as much as they should. The teacher expressed appreciation for this candid disclosure and suggested that they all give Patrick as much evidence as possible that they want to hear what he has to say. The advice turned out to have a major impact on Patrick, and he began to pay more attention to both his parents and teacher.

Of course, parents are not always so cooperative. Instead of being responsive to a teacher's concerns, parents may provide excuses for the child's behavior, or act as if they can't understand why the teacher could have these concerns. In this situation, the teacher needs to use the assertive communication skills we have described to persist with the concerns. It is especially important to avoid arguing with everything the parents say in defense of the child. Better results accrue from hearing what the parents have to say, acknowledging and empathizing with their point of view, and then refocusing the discussion on the concerns. If these tactics don't work, a teacher might let the matter go for the present and say, "Well, I'm still concerned about this. Let's see what happens in the next few weeks. I'll get back to you." This approach is preferable to one in which parents are forced into a corner by being asked, "What are *you* going to do about this problem?"

In contrast to a situation in which the teacher has concerns about students, parents often bring concerns about the teacher to a conference. This becomes particularly difficult when the parents express their concerns in an accusatory manner. For example, an irate father came to a conference demanding to know why the teacher let her students tease his daughter "mercilessly." Before waiting for an answer, he went on to accuse the teacher of indifference to the child's well-being. The teacher couldn't get a word in edgewise, so she switched gears and let the father talk rather than interrupt him with her viewpoint. Even when the father seemed to end his diatribe, she urged him to continue by saying, "I would like to know more about what your daughter told you about this problem and why you feel I'm being indifferent." Thus encouraged, the father went on for a long time until finally his anger was spent. Then the teacher quietly rebutted the father's perceptions of her indifference by explaining candidly that she was indeed concerned by the teasing, but beyond privately telling students to stop it, she had been unsure how to handle the matter. She suggested to the father two different approaches that might be taken. One attempted a quick but short-term solution and one involved a gradual, long-term solution. After some discussion, the father began to understand how difficult a problem like this is to solve and gave his support to the long-term solution. He also agreed to discuss with his daughter some ways she might handle the teasing in the meantime.

GETTING THE PRINCIPAL TO BE AN ALLY

Many of the things teachers need to do to gain the support of students, colleagues, and parents can be facilitated by an alliance with the principal or other appropriate administrative personnel. Therefore, it makes good sense for a teacher to explain to the principal how he or she can support the teacher's efforts. Even if a teacher is pessimistic about the principal's active support, it is not a good idea to act clandestinely. We remember a high school teacher who decided to put her plans and needs in a memo to the principal in advance of meeting with him face-to-face. Although the principal was reluctant to support the teacher's ideas (as she predicted), he was so impressed by the strength of her memo that he went along.

Perhaps the trickiest area of a relationship with a principal involves the handling of difficult behavior problems. Principals uniformly resent a teacher who constantly sends a classroom troublemaker to the school office, expecting thereby to be relieved of further responsibility for the child's antics. There is often good cause for principals to insist that the classroom teacher is the primary disciplinarian. After all, principals do not have a direct relationship with the classroom and thus, cannot deal with the problem between the teacher and the student as anything but a concerned outsider. Furthermore, the teacher's desire to have the principal assume responsibility is often self-defeating because the student may infer that the teacher's authority does not have any solid basis. She becomes just the teacher. Therefore, if a teacher wants to preserve the principal as an ally, she would do well to demonstrate that she takes charge of what happens in her classroom and exploits the principal's clout sparingly.

From time to time, however, a teacher reaches the limit with a misbehaving student. When this sense of desperation occurs, it certainly is reassuring to have the principal's backup help. For example, a seventh-grade teacher went to the principal after school one day totally at a loss for ideas to cope with an acting-out child in the classroom. The student had been not only disruptive in class for several weeks, but had successfully urged fellow students to be uncooperative as well. Sensing that the teacher was at wits' end, the principal asked how it would be possible to help. The teacher then suggested a three-step process: (1) the principal would meet with the student; (2) the principal would meet again with the teacher; and (3) a joint conference would be held with all three parties. The plan worked well. Because the principal was able to learn from the student some of the frustrations she was feeling in class, helpful advice could be given to the teacher to ameliorate the student's problems. At the same time, the teacher and the principal were able to forcefully demand during the three-way conference that the student cease her disruptions and conspiratorial activity.

Unfortunately some principals are almost never willing to back up the teacher's authority, either because they are too preoccupied with their administrative responsibilities to lend a helping hand, or because they succumb too easily to pressures from parents to lay off the troubled student. We have known teachers who report that every time they go to their principal for support, they are met with lame excuses about the principal's powerlessness in the matter or with guilt-inducing responses indicating that the teachers are placing an unfair burden on the principal. We usually counsel these teachers to believe in their right to seek the principal's intervention and to parry refusals with clear, honest expressions of how they feel about the lack of support. Initially, our advice is often rejected because the teachers also view themselves as powerless. But when we encourage them to persist, they are often surprised by their influence. Once they are able to confront the principal assertively, it is not uncommon for teachers to discover that the principal gains respect for their feelings and can wind up to be their best ally.

SUMMING UP

The list below summarizes all the suggestions we have provided to help cope with the fact that things are different in the classroom. Together, these ideas may be overwhelming to even the most ambitious teacher, but if one establishes some priorities, one would obtain some deserved support. One may, for example, choose to concentrate, for the time being, on those suggestions pertaining to a single source of support, and leave others to a later time.

- Help students get acquainted with each other.
- Plan an early activity to help give the entire class a sense of pride and accomplishment.
- Encourage students to help each other with their schoolwork.
- Evaluate your strengths and weaknesses as a stimulator, supporter, meaning-maker, and manager.

- Identify those long-term rules and policies you feel you must have for students.
- Swap experiences and ideas with other teachers on handling classroom discipline.
- Select a school-wide discipline problem which teachers can solve together.
- Request that a school counselor involve other teachers in a difficult problem you face with one of your students.
- Inform parents of your plans and expectations.
- Periodically send a newsletter to parents.
- Design a meaningful open house for parents and students.
- Involve parents in an effort to help you understand your students.
- Be open and assertive during parent conferences.
- Acquaint the principal with your ideas for getting support.
- Show the principal that you want primary responsibility for discipline.
- Suggest to the principal how you can be helped when you feel desperate.

Good luck with the suggestions you undertake!

11 | Overcoming Our Own Resistance to Change

A colleague of ours who has worked with parents and teachers for many years asked us a very serious and challenging question about this book: "There are many books that offer sound advice for teachers and parents. How will this book be any different? No matter what suggestions are offered, I rarely see any real change in the way parents and teachers deal with children. People never change, or they change just enough not to change at all."

Our colleague makes a valid point. Most of us want to change parts of our behavior but thwart our own efforts in many ways. How many diets, New Year's resolutions and other plans to change do we actually carry out? We may make such resolutions sincerely, but return to our previous patterns quite easily. Change takes work but as an old saying goes, "Most human beings would rather lie under a tree and stare at the sky." And change means giving up some of the comfort, certainty, and rewards that we get from our current behavior.

One way that we keep ourselves from changing is to deny that a problem exists and therefore choose not to see the need for change. When we allow ourselves to face a problem, we often must also face our fears, and no one likes to do that. It's easier to bury our heads in the sand fearing that if we really look into the situation, our suspicions might be confirmed; something might be

189

wrong. We even may fear that dealing with a problem could make it worse. These kinds of concerns can lead to wishful thinking: Don't discuss it, leave it alone and it will go away. Unfortunately, most situations don't go away, but become more problematic and serious because we deny them. Some examples:

A sixth-grade teacher notices that a student speaks so softly that it's almost impossible to hear her. The child's writing is so small that one needs a magnifying glass to read it. The child speaks to no one, but her work is done well and on time. She is always very polite and courteous. Another teacher suggests that this child may be in need of counseling, but the original teacher does not see this child as having a problem. The child is shy, but she is also a good, well-behaved child.

The parents of a teen-age boy have noticed that their son has a scale, an inordinate number of sandwich bags in his room, and what looks like seeds on his rug. He also received an extraordinary number of phone calls—many from adults. Neither parent mentions these things to their son or to each other. When their son is arrested for selling marijuana, they are stunned and can't believe that their son could be involved in such activities. The police have obviously made a mistake.

When we deny problems we lose, and the children in our care lose. First of all, ignoring a problem may be seen by children as approval of their behavior. Secondly, children may decide that we don't care about them and escalate their misbehavior in order to get us to realize that they need our help. Drug overdoses are, in many cases, an attempt by a child to get the assistance of parents and teachers. Less dramatic events such as temper tantrums, fighting, stealing, or failure at school may also be clues from children that they need help. Denial of a problem is often a denial of adult responsibility. It is, in effect, a denial of the child's right to adult guidance.

Even when we are aware of a need to change the way we're dealing with a child, we may resist taking action because we feel that the situation is somehow our fault. If a child is experiencing problems, we assume that we must be inadequate teachers or parents, we feel guilty that things aren't going well, and we take responsibility for the child's actions. For example, a parent who is guilt-ridden about a teen-ager's truancy might think: "We've always been too easy on him, but it's too late for us to change." A teacher faced with a child who is often unprepared for class could dismiss the behavior by thinking: "He has such a difficult home life. I feel horrible when I ask him where his homework is."

When we believe that the problem is our fault, or the fault of society, we usually deny ourselves the right to exercise our authority, to demand responsible behavior, or to discipline the children in our care. Our guilt may translate into being kind and lenient with a child who, in fact, needs limits and guidance. We let things slide and feel noble about it. Again, we lose and the child loses.

Anger is another source of resistance to working on situations. Sometimes we believe that if we tried to deal with a problem, our anger at the child would cause us to overreact, explode, or become physically abusive. Examples of such feelings are: "If I say anything to him, I'll start yelling and lose control" or, "I can't deal with her. If I try, I'll kill her."

Fear of losing control typically results in inaction; we may conclude that it's better to do nothing than to react violently toward a child. It's as if our feelings are in charge of our actions and that the only way to control ourselves is to not do anything about the situation.

Another possible source of resistance is a sense of futility. When we try things that don't work, we may subtly begin to perceive ourselves or the child as incapable of change. This sense of futility can be very energy-draining and will perpetuate inaction because we believe that nothing we try will have any effect. We may then find ourselves using such words as *uncontrollable, incorrigible,* or *unteachable* to describe the child. Or we may begin to think of ourselves as incapable of exerting control or unable to cope with the situation. However, the more we think in these terms, the less likely we are to act.

Finally, we can thwart our efforts to change by doing more of what hasn't worked in the past. If our solution isn't working, we may try even harder to make that same solution work. All of us engage in this type of problem solving because, in some cases, trying harder at the same solution works. If we have an argument with a teen-ager, for example, and end up not speaking to each other for several days, it seems logical to break the norm of silence and begin to talk again. This often works. The situation (silence) is corrected by applying more of the same solution (talking). In many cases, though, a teacher or parent will try to talk to the teen-ager only to be met with more silence. Because the initial attempt to change the situation didn't succeed, the adult attempts to start conversations with the teen-ager more often. When this doesn't work, more attempts are made and met with even more resistance. By now the reasons for the initial argument are forgotten. The problem now might be stated by the adult in these terms: "She won't talk to me. I've tried everything, but she doesn't confide in me anymore. I can't reach her." What happens in such instances is that rather than attempting another solution, the same solution is employed with more vigor which compounds, instead of solves, the initial problem.

Sometimes we get stuck pursuing the same old solution simply because we can't think of anything else to do. Most of us are not trained in problem solving and rely on our past experiences to solve problems. Once a solution is chosen and attempted, it's difficult to back up and look for another answer. By the time we realize that our initial solution doesn't work, we may be involved in a persistent pattern with a child. These patterns, or vicious cycles, are hard to break. We want to get off the merry-go-round but fear that trying something different may make it worse.

CHANGING SELF-STATEMENTS

As we have noted, our resistance to taking steps to change our behavior can come from the way we think about things. Guilt feelings, fear of destructive anger, and thinking of the child or of oneself as incapable of change are all examples of things which prevent one from being assertive and dealing directly with a problem situation. One key to overcoming this resistance, then, is to change our statements from *self-defeating* ones to *self-enhancing* ones. As simple as this sounds, it is valid to claim that accentuating the positive provides more energy to find and to try creative solutions to problems. Examples of changing how we think about such situations are:

- "I'm so angry I could kill him," can be changed to, "If I do something about this, my anger will subside."
- "How can I expect him to do well in school. His homelife is so deprived," can become a positive thought: "By helping

him do better in school, he may develop a good strong sense of self."

- "I should try to do something but I just can't bring myself to discipline her," can be phrased without resistance: "If I take action, she'll know that I care about her."

ATTACKING IRRATIONAL BELIEFS

Yet another way to help us think more positively has been outlined by Albert Ellis,* the proponent of Rational Emotive Therapy. Ellis has devised a useful five-step strategy to assess thoughts and to examine their effect on feelings and behaviors. Step 1 involves identifying the situation about which we feel upset. For example:
"My classroom is too noisy. I want the children to be more quiet and attentive."
Step 2 is to look at a belief we have about that situation which may be irrational. For example: "If I try, but fail, to get the children to be more attentive, I'm an ineffective teacher and my peers and principal will know it."
Step 3 involves asking ourselves what emotional reaction we have to the thoughts in steps 1 and 2. For example: "I feel depressed, anxious, and scared."
It is at this point that many people get stuck and are unable to take action. Ellis suggests that we challenge the irrational belief (Step 4): "What if I try and it doesn't work? Other teachers have trouble keeping order in their classrooms. My principal knows that it's hard to effectively discipline children. I won't be ridiculed and, even if I am, I'll survive."
Step 5 urges the substitution of more rational thoughts to replace their irrational counterparts. For example: "I'll give it a try. It would be terrific if my plan works but, if it doesn't, I'll live. I'll simply try another plan."
When faced with a situation toward which we feel resistant, going through these steps can help identify and change the thoughts that are preventing us from acting. Once we begin to think more positively, we'll feel more hopeful. This will give us the push we need to begin to formulate potential solutions to problems.

*Albert Ellis, *Disrupting Irrational Beliefs*. (New York: Institute for Rational Living, 1974).

DEVELOPING A PERSONAL CHANGE STRATEGY

For the times when positive thinking and attacking our irrational beliefs are not sufficient, we can use a personal change strategy that helps us break old patterns and create new ones.

This strategy can be used again and again as different situations arise in which you feel stuck. Although it is clearly not necessary for all situations, it does provide a systematic way to see your problem more clearly and to find alternative ways to solve it. We also see the plan as a vehicle to help you integrate what you've gained from this book.

STEP I: GOAL IDENTIFICATION AND CONCRETIZATION

Briefly describe a situation that you've encountered with your child(ren) or student(s). Choose a situation that occurs frequently and that you would like to change. The situation should be one in which you are not satisfied with the present outcome and in which you would like to change *your* behavior. (The idea is that the child's behavior may change if you change.) Take some time to answer these questions:

1. What actually happens?
2. Who are you with when it happens?
3. How often does the situation occur?
4. How do you react psychologically? Physically?
5. What do you gain by behaving the way you do in the situation? (For example, by being nonassertive, you might avoid conflict.)
6. How you would like the situation to be different?

Now go back and describe more clearly the situation that you've chosen to work on by filling in the blanks below.

1. I understand the situation specifically to be that

_____

_____

2. I would like the situation to change in the following way:

_____

_____

STEP II: EXAMINATION OF INTERNAL AND EXTERNAL FACTORS
MAINTAINING THE PROBLEM SITUATION

When a problem situation exists, there are usually forces at work in you to maintain the status quo. There are reasons why you want to change the situation and reasons why you don't want to change the situation. For example, if your situation is that you want your children, ages 11 and 12, to clean their rooms every Saturday morning and you've been telling them to do this without success for three months, there could be a number of forces affecting you in the situation.

Forces pushing you toward accomplishing this goal might be that:

- You want your home to be kept neat.
- You believe that parents should teach children to be neat and clean.
- You work and don't have time to clean the room(s) yourself.
- You don't want to have to nag these children every Saturday for eight more years.
- You value cooperation among family members to get household chores done.

Forces keeping you from changing your behavior in this situation might be:

- You don't like the hassle of keeping after the children until the room(s) are clean.
- You don't want your children to feel like maids.
- You know that it would take less time to do it yourself than to supervise the job.
- You tend to back down to avoid a conflict when your kids argue with you.
- You don't seem to know what to say or do differently to change the situation and so you approach the situation feeling anxious and intimidated.

The net result in this situation would most likely be that you would continue to tell the children every Saturday to clean their rooms and they would continue to ignore your request. Although some forces may have more impact on you than others, a stalemate occurs if the strength of the forces for change are equal to or less than the forces against change. *The best way to break this stalemate is to reduce the effect of the forces keeping you from changing.*

Returning to your situation, list the forces driving you toward wanting to change the situation:

a. _____

b. _____

c. _____

d. _____

e. _____

List the forces keeping you from attempting to change the situation:

a. _____

b. _____

c. _____

d. _____

e. _____

STEP III: THE DEVELOPMENT OF AN ACTION PLAN

By now you have a pretty clear understanding of what is maintaining the problem situation that you have chosen to work on. It's time to make an action plan.

Choose two or three of the forces holding you back, perhaps those in which you have some confidence that change is possible. Try to think of as many ways as possible to reduce the hold that these forces have on you. Let your imagination flow with as many ideas as possible. You might also leaf through this book for ideas.

In your hypothetical situation you could: clean the room yourself, say nothing, learn to deal with conflict more constructively, develop a reward system for the children when they clean the room, or find a more effective way to communicate what you want.

When you list alternatives, don't judge them as you go along. After you've generated alternatives, you can decide which ones will be best for you to try. In this example, saying nothing or cleaning the room yourself may not be the best alternatives if they don't reduce your feelings of frustration or anger at your children. Instead, you may decide to work on dealing with conflict and developing a reward system.

STEP IV: PRIORITIZING YOUR IDEAS

As you can see, even a simple problem situation may require learning a number of new skills and attitudes in order to solve the problem. You know now what you need to do, but you can't do everything at once. A plan of attack is needed. Our hypothetical parent might want to practice ways to minimize conflict first. Then, she or he might want to work on stating expectations and consequences clearly. Finally, the parent might choose to develop a system of rewards for the children. It would be helpful for you to sequence the ideas you try by filling in the blanks below.

I plan to work on these ideas to reduce some forces that block me from changing:

1. _____

2. _____

3. _____

Although it takes time to develop an action plan, the payoff is worthwhile. An action plan will help you to identify more clearly what the problem is, to clarify the reasons for the stalemate you may be experiencing, and to feel more capable of handling the situation.

In implementing your action plan, you might use some of the ideas and techniques outlined in this book. You may also find it helpful to enlist the aid of other people in carrying out your plan. As you begin to implement the plan, ask your children to help you evaluate how well the plan is working. Working at change together creates a spirit of cooperation in them and a support system for you. Finally, be persistent in your efforts to change your behavior and applaud yourself, as we do, for your willingness to be in charge.

Further Reading

Assertion

Alberti, R. E., ed. *Assertiveness: Innovations, Applications, Issues.* San Luis Obispo, Calif.: Impact Publishers, 1977.

Alberti, R. E., and Emmons, M. L. *Your Perfect Right: A Guide to Assertive Behavior.* San Luis Obispo, Calif.: Impact Publishers, 1974.

Cotler, S. B., and Guerra, J. J. *Assertion Training: A Humanistic-Behavioral Guide to Self-Dignity.* Champaign, Ill.: Research Press, 1976.

Fensterheim, H., and Baer, J. *Don't Say Yes When You Want to Say No.* New York: Dell Publishing Co., 1975.

Galassi, M. E., and Galassi, J. P. *Assert Yourself! How to Be Your Own Person.* New York: Human Science Press, 1977.

Lange, A. J., and Jakubowski, P. *Responsible Assertive Behavior: Cognitive/Behavioral Procedures for Trainers.* Champaign, Ill.: Research Press, 1976.

Smith, M. J. *When I Say No, I Feel Guilty.* New York: Bantam Books, 1975.

Discipline

Bartz, W. R., and Rasor, R. A. *Surviving with Kids.* Illustrated by R. Pike. San Luis Obispo, Calif.: Impact Publishers, 1978.

Dobson, J. *Dare to Discipline*. New York: Bantam Books, 1977.

Dreikurs, R. *Children. The Challenge*. New York: Hawthorn Books, 1964.

Hersey, P., and Blanchard, K. H. *The Family Game: A Situational Approach to Effective Parenting*. Reading, Mass.: Addison–Wesley Publishing Co., 1978.

Kiley, D. *Nobody Said It Would Be Easy*. New York: Harper & Row, 1978.

Schaefer, C. *How to Influence Children: A Handbook of Practical Parenting Skills*. New York: Van Nostrand Reinhold Co., 1978.

Smith, J. M., and Smith, D. E. P. *Child Management: A Program for Parents and Teachers*. Champaign, Ill.: Research Press, 1976.

Tanner, L. *Classroom Discipline for Effective Teaching and Learning*. New York: Holt, Rinehart & Winston, 1978.

Wood, P., and Schwartz, B. *How to Get Your Children to Do What You Want Them to Do*. Englewood Cliffs: Prentice–Hall, Inc., 1977.

Wood, S.; Bishop, R.; and Cohen, D. *Parenting: Four Patterns of Child-Rearing*. New York: Hart Publishing Co., 1978.

Parents Alone

Atkin, E., and Rubin, E. *Part-Time Father*. New York: Signet Books, 1977.

Galper, M. *Co-Parenting: A Sourcebook for the Separated or Divorced Family*. Philadelphia: Running Press, 1978.

Gardner, R. A. *The Parents Book About Divorce*. New York: Doubleday, 1977.

Hoffman, L., and Nye, F. I. *Working Mothers*. San Francisco: Josey Bass, Inc., 1974.

Hope, K., and Young, N., eds., *Momma: The Sourcebook for Single Mothers*. New York: New American Library, 1976.

Levine, J. A. *Who Will Raise the Children? New Options for Fathers (and Mothers)*. New York: Bantam Books, 1977.

Rosenbaum, J., and Rosenbaum, V. *Stepparenting*. New York: E.P. Dutton, 1978.

Therapy and Family Process

Arnold, L. E. *Helping Parents Help Their Children*. New York: Brunner/Mazel, Publishers, 1978.

Ellis, A. *Humanistic Psychotherapy: The Rational-Emotive Approach*. New York: Julian Press, 1974.

Haley, J. *Uncommon Therapy: The Psychiatric Techniques of Milton H. Erickson, M.D.* New York: W. W. Norton & Co., 1973.

Glasser, W. *Reality Therapy: A New Approach to Psychiatry.* New York: Harper & Row, Publishers, 1965, 1975.

Lazurus, A. A. *Behavior Therapy and Beyond.* New York: McGraw–Hill, 1971.

Minuchin, S. *Families and Family Therapy.* Cambridge: Harvard University Press, 1974.

Satir, V. *Peoplemaking.* Palo Alto, Calif.: Science and Behavior Books, Inc., 1972.

Group Building

Bany, M. A., and Johnson, L. V. *Educational Social Psychology.* New York: Macmillan Publishing Co., Inc., 1975.

Glasser, W. *Schools Without Failure.* New York: Harper & Row, 1972.

Howe, L., and Howe, M. *Personalizing Education: Values Clarification and Beyond.* New York: Hart Publishing Co., 1975.

Johnson, D. W., and Johnson, R. T. *Learning Together and Alone: Cooperation, Competition, and Individualization.* Englewood Cliffs: Prentice–Hall, Inc., 1975.

Schmuck, R. A., and Schmuck, P. A. *Group Processes in the Classroom* 3d ed. Dubuque, Iowa: William C. Brown, Co., 1979.

Silberman, M. L.; Allender, J. S.; and Yanoff, J. A., eds. *Real Learning: A Sourcebook for Teachers.* Boston: Little Brown & Co., 1976.

Stanford, G. *Developing Effective Classroom Groups: A Practical Guide for Teachers.* New York: Hart Publishing Co., 1977.

Training for Assertive Relations With Children

Dr. Silberman and Dr. Wheelan conduct training programs based on the philosophy and techniques in *How To Discipline Without Feeling Guilty*. Workshops are offered for professionals who themselves individually counsel or conduct groups for parents or teachers on discipline problems. Programs and courses for anyone who cares directly for children—from toddlers to teens—are also available.

FOR INFORMATION ABOUT TRAINING FOR ASSERTIVE RELATIONSHIPS WITH CHILDREN, WRITE TO:

THE ARC PROGRAM—Assertive Relations With Children
120 W. Lancaster Ave.
Ardmore, Pennsylvania 19003
(215) 649-6400

Index

203

Dr. Melvin L. Silberman received his Ph.D. in educational psychology from the University of Chicago in 1968 and trained as a family therapist at the Philadelphia Child Guidance Clinic. He has previously edited three books— *The Experience of Schooling, The Psychology of Open Teaching and Learning,* and *Real Learning*—and has conducted a wide range of assertion training workshops for parents, teachers, social workers, government employees, nurses, and mental health practitioners. He is currently Professor of Psychoeducational Processes at Temple University and co-director of THE ARC PROGRAM—Assertive Relations With Children.

Dr. Susan A. Wheelan received her Ph.D. in educational psychology from the University of Wisconsin in 1974. She is currently Associate Professor of Psychoeducational Processes at Temple University and is a licensed psychologist in Pennsylvania and co director of THE ARC PROGRAM— Assertive Relations With Children. A nationally known consultant in human relations and a specialist in assertion training, she has authored several articles on nonassertion and depression, the change process, and sexism in human relations training.